PLAYS

Conversations After a Burial
Théâtre Paris-Villette, Théâtre Montparnasse (1987);
Almeida Theatre, London (2000)

The Passage of Winter
Théâtre du Rond-Pont, Paris (1990)

Art
Comédie des Champs-Élysées (1994);
Wyndham's Theatre, London (1996);
Royale Theater, New York (1999)

The Unexpected Man
Théâtre Hébertot, Paris (1996);
Royal Shakespeare Company and Duchess Theatre,
London (1998); Promenade Theater, New York (2000)

Life x 3
Burgtheater, Vienna (2000); Théâtre Antoine, Paris (2000);
National Theatre, London (2000)

OTHER WORKS

A translation of Steven Berkoff's version of Kafka's
Metamorphosis, directed by Roman Polanski
Hammerklavier, a novel
Desolation, a novel
Adam Haberberg, a novel
Lulu Kreutz's Picnic, a film, directed by Didier Martiny

Dawn, Dusk or Night

Dawn, Dusk or Night

A YEAR WITH NICOLAS SARKOZY

Yasmina Reza

TRANSLATED FROM THE FRENCH
BY THE AUTHOR AND PIERRE GUGLIELMINA

Alfred A. Knopf   *New York*   2008

Library of Congress Cataloging-in-Publication Data
Reza, Yasmina.
[Aube le soir ou la nuit. English]
Dawn, dusk or night / by Yasmina Reza ; translated from the
French by Pierre Guglielmina and Yasmina Reza.—1st U.S. ed.
ISBN 978-0-307-26921-8
p. cm.
1. Sarkozy, Nicolas, 1955– 2. Statesmen—France—Biography.
3. France—Politics and government—1995–2007. I. Title.
DC433.R4913 2008
944.084092—dc22
[B]   2007047242

Manufactured in the United States of America

First American Edition

For G.

Dawn, Dusk or Night

Man alone is a dream. Man alone is an illusion. One likes to think of them in an emblematic solitude, but men only pretend to be alone. This is deceiving. Predators, they are called, but predators are solitary. Without doubt, within their territory, men can be predatory. Elsewhere, they are tame.

In the office at Place Beauvau, where we meet for the first time, he listens graciously, and then I very quickly perceive, in little ways, something with which I am all too familiar, impatience.

He has understood. He is "honored" that I would

like to do his portrait. He says, So, you want to be there. I say, Yes.

Later, I am talking with my friend Marc in a café.

Anyway, you'll reinvent him. Writers, like tyrants, are capable of bending the world to their will.

No landscape. No city. For a long time, I will not see a thing. Not a place, not even him.

Thus, this day, a highway through nowhere. Road signs, exit. Warehouses. Venue. Headlong rush into the dressing room. Constant stream of things to nibble. In the prefabricated makeup room, some prunes, some chocolate, candied fruit squares. Him nibbling constantly. Nibbling, gobbling, rushing. I had noticed that he ate fast, just as I had noticed that he limped.

Getting dressed, after the meeting in Agen, he keeps repeating, They want to cut down on the working hours, when we want to boost the purchasing power. He has said it during the speech, in front of six thousand people—had said it solemnly the night before, during the dinner, in his apartment at the Ministère (with a slightly ridiculous solemnity, as if seriously testing). He repeats the sentence over and over to these people he has no need to convince, he is happy, he

repeats the words as he changes his shirt, still in disbe-
lief, still waiting, like a child, for the umpteenth
approval.

In front of André Glucksmann* asking questions
(twenty-five minutes each, in a slow and didactic
voice) on Europe's future, EU energy policy, or the
fate of Africa, he slouches in his chair, upper body
projecting patience, legs restless, opening and closing
in perpetual motion.

As the Bastille Day garden party winds down, he is
hugging Christian Clavier.† They are hugging the way
actors do. Wild with joy, with love, with You, I mean
you, my pal, shouted at the whole world. The kind of
hug I have seen a thousand times, other places, other
faces, actors hell-bent on hugging publicly, drunk
with their own performance, with their demonstrative
laughter, their superhuman zeal. A little bit later, as he
is burying his tie in the black bag he is taking to Rome,
he says to me, Did you see who was there? Did you
see? . . . No . . . Mathias's parents. (Mathias? . . .) Mathias, if I remember correctly, was the little boy who was

* French philosopher and writer.
† French actor.

raped and murdered. The day before, during a conversation on foreign policy with Glucksmann and Bruckner,* he had managed to slip in the Mathias story—he had mentioned it to me at some point, I don't know when. Mathias's parents. Mathias's parents were there. I nod in sympathy. What else do you do?

Flipping through *Le Point* the day his book, *Testimony,* comes out. Alongside the excerpts, some photos captioned and perhaps chosen by him. As is usually the case, and well before I met him, I am struck by the childhood. Childhood, intelligence, men's clothing. The tie and the suit never fit his age. The man's suit accentuating a kind of fragility. The laugh is not the laugh of someone his age. He seems more elegant these days. I say so to Pierre Charon.† He is elegant, yes, he's gone back to Dior. Before, he wore Lanvin, Lanvin is normally the thing, but it has to be tailored, the sleeves cut, all kinds of alterations, Dior suits him better.

.   .   .

* Pascal Bruckner, French writer of the left, who nonetheless supported the 2003 invasion of Iraq.

† Communications consultant for Sarkozy's presidential campaign.

Observing him at the town hall in Palavas-les-Flots* as he listens to someone introduce his speech, I feel like I'm watching a little boy. Standing, hands clasped, waiting politely.

In the car, Bernard Fixot, his publisher, whispers, He has changed a lot. He thinks about himself, about who he is. It's hard to stop long enough to think: I'm doing this, and why am I doing this? That's not easy for a man of action. He has evolved, Fixot continues. He is more solid, more authentic. (His entourage makes a point of praising him to me unreservedly.) I ask, Since when? But I don't get a clear answer.

Often, he says, How you doin', Yasmina? But that means, How is he doing? How you doin', Yasmina, happy? You saw that crowd, huh? . . .

In the plane, after pressing-the-flesh on the beach in 110° weather and the book signing, he says, People are nice . . . You saw. And the number of people who say, Give Cécilia a kiss for me! I say, You too, you're nice. He dismisses what I say, The people, they come and what, I'm going to curse them out?

* Port Sunshine.

. . .

The people he is talking about are well dressed in this bookstore, in the middle of a thousand-degree summer. Pretty dresses, necklaces, makeup, only a few men in shorts. They stand in line for two hours. Thank you, Jean-Paul, heh. Go, go for it. I'm gonna go for it, Alain, all the way. Look at your mother, Jean-Baptiste (she is trying to take a picture with her cell phone upside down), if you don't, we're both gonna get it. I admire you, sir, more than I can say. I see it, Solange, that works for me. You're going to win. We're going to try, Marie-Ange. Leaving, on the street, in the nuclear heat of noon, a bunch of arms wave open books. He signs a few more on the cover page.

People, a procession of first names. Voices, hands, already left behind.

On the plane going home. "It's mostly women who come. They see the sensitivity! . . . And all to make Bernard Fixot a richer man!" We laugh. They congratulate themselves on the morning's win. Again and again. Repeating that it went well. Repeating before it fades away.

. . .

G., who inspired this book and who nourishes the same ambition, has said to me, One has to find a way to fill the day.

To a taxi driver, Place Beauvau, please, the Ministry of the Interior. My, my! Me, an Arab, you're taking me to Sarkozy's!

He begins the staff meeting, on his feet, pacing around his chair. You don't end a letter with My salutations! Who ends a letter with My salutations? Salutations is such a tacky word. Warm salutations. That's worse than a form letter from Social Security. My warm salutations! Unbelievable. Just to sign a letter, they have to show it to me three times!

In Luc Bondy's* book, there is an enigmatic sentence: "too much leads *straight* to death." Earlier in his book, he writes about living too much. What does it mean to live too much? Seemingly, I have always written on the polar opposite. From the polar opposite. From the monotony, the minutes falling into the void, the feeling of a world amiss. Scores of sentences on desire exceeding what is delivered, scores of hymns to impatience.

---

* Swiss theater and opera director.

During the meeting, listening to his staffers, one after another, smoking a cigar, left leg on the table, right leg moving, he suffers no explanation, no useless clarification. So what is the conclusion?

To the Prefecture, during a meeting on the immigration law, he announces vehemently, There are a dozen prefectures where I reckon I am being mocked. If you don't want to apply the measures of this government, find another job. It's not a question of right or left, it's a question of law.

From first jotted notes, he says this, he does that. Is it new? Is it normal for him? I have no clue.

It always ends badly, says Ivan. In France, there is no term limit for political life, if one steps down, it is because one is sick, old, or defeated. Hence, fallen.

In politics, there is no such thing as *the end of a beautiful day.*

Another day, Marc came to this conclusion, that in matters of the heart, a single loss is worth forty wins. Loss foretells that which is to come.

In Lausanne, on a gently sloped street, under a glorious sun, a woman in her early sixties is waiting patiently, sitting at a bus stop. The street is a bit deserted on this summer day, maybe every day, a quiet street with low buildings. The woman is well dressed, she is sitting upright, neatly groomed. She is waiting unassumingly for the bus, she is going to visit a friend (I can just imagine too the Swiss apartment, tidy and a little dark) or to have lunch with a relative, her daughter, her son . . . She too fills her day.

Finding a way to fill the day, in the words of G., means to put oneself out there. Could you imagine him, seated alone, waiting there where nothing moves?

The man, whom I now scrutinize and won't bring myself to name, cannot remain still, either. Though the isolation revealed in some pictures, some photographs, is arresting. (Striking enough to inspire these lines too).

Summer separates. I see him from afar. In the papers, on television. I see him in London, on France 2, in Arcachon . . . He seems subdued to me, no fight left in him, winded. The mind is prone to embellish, to walk the tightrope of hypothesis. His rival now (and in the future?), she is all smiles, radiant, fierce.

Jorge Luis Borges has written the most beautiful words on lovers torn apart. He whose writing is the least sentimental, he who in his work barely touches on the subject of love.

A few sentences, scarce, threaded through swords, daggers, blades of all kinds.

> The only thing that is ours is what we have lost.
>
> Ours are the women who have left us, at long last indifferent to expectation, which is anxiety, and to the alarms and terrors of hope.

> (. . .) I am trying to bride you with uncertainty, with danger, with defeat.

The poets have the privilege of obeying untimely laws, which require neither logic nor, apparently, follow-through. These laws serve a truth that all explanation would betray.

That liberty, I take here.

New York.

The Engine 54, Ladder 4 firehouse seems tiny like a toy. Large white tiles all around, a basketball hoop on the back wall. From that firehouse, on September 11, 2001, fifteen firemen left, never to return. The gleaming and surreal truck brings to mind, I don't know why, this picture where we see him holding a miniature police car from the fifties. He smiles the awkward smile of a child showing off a gift. In his address for the anniversary, on this day, he quotes the lyrics of "Into the Fire" by Bruce Springsteen, *May your strength give us strength, may your faith give us faith . . .* with an appalling accent. During the brief Medal of Honor ceremony for the New York firemen, a real child is standing at his side, just ten years old and nearly as tall as he. The fatherless silent hero of the moment goes through the motions as instructed, completely ignorant of this foreign dignitary who has come to pay his respects.

When I tell his entourage that he looks like a child, I get stunned stares.

Lunching in The Pierre, I explain my project to a businessman sitting across from me. I say, I am not looking to write on power or on politics, but rather on politics as a way of being. I'm more interested in watching a man who intends to trump time. Nicolas (I say his name!) seems delighted, gratified that I put it that way. He jokes familiarly, I kinda get who you are, I could write a book about you myself.

.   .   .

In the course of the same lunch, talking about teen-agers, he says, They have to become independent, they have to. The problem is when they become independent and not nice, nice is more important.

Words that do not stand out, although they are the first that I hear from his mouth to denote a personal life.

She's writing that down! he laughs, seeing me pull a pad out of my bag. I say, I have to write that one down.

Bragging. What other adjective could I choose to describe him at the French consulate meeting representatives of the major Jewish organizations? Maybe he is right, Jews have no particular affinity with modesty. "I am number one in the polls in spite of the fact I am a friend of America and of Israel. I don't want to sound pretentious. I'm fifty-one and I'm unfazed. Don't get wrapped up in articles by stupid journalists who don't understand anything. Part of the French elite detests me a lot more than they detest Israel or the Americans." At the end of the encounter, he stands up as he is questioned about his future, eight months ahead of the presidential election. "We can pray," says Israel Singer, president of the executive committee of the World Jewish Congress, the only person in the assembly wearing a yarmulke. "Pray, yes . . ." he murmurs, lowering his head.

In Washington, in a small office of the French American Foundation, sitting on a sofa, he is listening to Ambassador Jean-David Levitte. For the first time, I see him absorbing information without impatience and with no intention of responding. Subtle movements of the legs, discreet undulation. Levitte talks to him about senators Obama and McCain, and about President Bush. Being a Texan, says Levitte, Bush operates on friendship. Schröder betrayed him. Angela Merkel has figured out what to do. Angela did what you are doing. She had established a personal relationship before her election. He will appear poised and warm, adds Levitte, but behind the facade you will discover a man in a state of great disarray.

He only likes the city, says Jean-Michel Goudard,* he doesn't like the countryside, going around meeting people, he has to do it, but it bugs the shit out of him! For starters, he doesn't like trains. Things he doesn't like, he does to the letter. If you tell him, We need

*French publicity executive with BBDO Japan who worked for the Sarkozy campaign in 2007.

to see more of you, he is going to prance around in his boxers. He says, People like me being me, why change?

They sit, facing each other, two men both intending to be presidents one day.

Our integration policy doesn't work at all. A senator like you, advisers like Condi Rice or Colin Powell don't exist in France. My opponents say, He is going to take his orders from the United States. Since I saw Bush this morning, it's important that I see you this afternoon. That balances it.

Looking up, one sees Abraham Lincoln, Martin Luther King, Gandhi, J. F. Kennedy laughing with some black musicians. In the office of the splendid Barack Obama, the idea of America itself is hanging on the walls.

What makes you different from George Bush?

How am I different from Bush? He was elected president of the United States twice.

None of the journalists present in the room at the Sofitel seems to appreciate the intelligence of this response, and I will not see it quoted anywhere in the French press.

. . .

Faster. Farther. Each place wiping out the one before. Not even places. Just names of places, hotels, quixotic sites, UN, Capitol, White House, dashing through, hallways, offices, strategic handshakes exchanged for the front page. That's New York. That's Washington. That's life.

In *Testimony,* he writes: "Today, Cécilia and I have gotten back together for real, and surely forever." I confess to Catherine Pégard* not having understood the statement; in a book, a long-lasting medium, isn't it risky to expose oneself like that, out of pure pride? My naïveté surprises her. So what? she says, there is no truth other than now.

Boulevard Raspail, I bump into Eric Neuhoff.† I confirm the rumor he has heard. (As I write these first lines, everybody seems to be surprised by my approach.)

Don't do it, Yasmina, he says in a friendly and earnest tone.

But you don't know what I'm doing.

---

* French political journalist and editor who worked at *Le Point* magazine before becoming an adviser to Sarkozy in mid-May 2007.
† Author and screenwriter.

Don't do it, Yasmina, they are stronger than us.

When we part, I think back on this and on the word "stronger." To be threatened by someone's strength, you have to be in competition with him.

Or weakened by sentiment.

I don't believe that the Minister of the Interior is stronger than I.

Often I hear, "upon assuming the supreme power" . . . People often talk to me about the *supreme power*. Why is it so difficult to consider the presidency of the French Republic as the supreme power? If not, what else would be? Assuming the possibility of such a thing in this world.

On television, I don't recognize G. He keeps saying, I want . . . I want . . . I'm the one who . . . I'm best positioned to . . . he says *I* every chance he gets. The G. I know is reticent and secretive. It pains me to listen to him.

"I seek silence and the night when I want to cry," says Chimène in *Le Cid*. The men I observe are looking for the contrary. Definitely not the night, certainly not the silence. Least of all, the tears. Nothing to mark *time*.

. . .

On the plane taking us to Lozère, he gives us the sales figures of his book. A number so precise, almost disturbing in its detail. I point it out to him, he agrees with a chuckle.

Yes, it's sick. I look at the sales, the returns, I like net figures, imprecision bothers me. The publisher faxes me every day. It might be the definition of mania. Actually, it's a drug. Sometimes, I even request regional breakdowns!

A few days before, he and Cécilia attended a performance of *In Arthur Schopenhauer's Toboggan*. He brings it up during the flight and, for the benefit of all, recites a line from the script . . . *I force myself to draw up my body so that it leans in closer to yours, so that you might decipher this obscure movement, this minute orientation of angle . . .* an essential line, rarely noticed.

In Rieutort-de-Randon, on the village square, a small gathering of men in ties (I will never again see so many crazy ties), in military caps, rustic garb, women in their Sunday best or aprons, children. The sun is out, he shakes hands, hugs people, some say, I pray for you, he answers, It can't hurt, he signs autographs, poses for some family photos, they cheer him on, he responds, thank you, thank you, huh. I would like to linger on this "huh" I keep hearing and on the ring it has. As if the exclamation were more a cover than a crutch for the word. Is there regret in this "huh," something he is not aware of or would not know how to say, a sparse apology for time he cannot spare, for fleeting contact brutally severed?

Or perhaps nothing.

On his way out of Lolo's butcher shop, he says, pointing at a remarkably banal donkey poster, Nice ass.

A man in the crowd:

Oh, come on, let's have a drink now! Once he's president, he won't be back here.

He says two things on the plane taking us back to Paris.

I am CRAZY about Chimène Badi.*

It might surprise you, but I don't think that Dick Rivers† is a moron.

* Young French-Algerian singer, also the winner of a French reality show called *Popstars*.

† French singer and actor (born Hervé Forneri), who has been performing since the early 1960s and helped introduce rock and roll to France.

. . .

After popular music, we move on to more familiar ground. He says, One day, I'll write in a book what my ambition prevented me from saying.

Several times, I have heard him say, When I am done with ambition.

In midair where we find ourselves on that twenty-seventh of October 2006, he repeats, ambition is not the ultimate thing, there is life after ambition. I don't doubt his sincerity but I do doubt the likelihood that his ambition could burn out and his life not fade away. He objects that I am confusing ambition with desire (he is right, but we don't give the same meaning to the word "ambition.")

I want to retrace his words, in this very real conversation, the first one we really have (and in which I finally use the familiar "tu" rather than "vous" with him).

"Ambition transforms desire into something incandescent, he says. There are moments when I aspire to a little less incandescence. Look, I have everything I could ever want, I dreamed of having a party, I have it, I dreamed of getting the best government posts, I got them, I dreamed to be the right man in the right place at the right time, and I am. But I'm over that. It's rough. We're already there, in office. I'm not in the *before* anymore."

"When I was young, I thought, Everything is possible. Everything was against me, but I thought, Everything is possible."

Word for word, I could say the same.

November. Under the cold sun, a black whorl of cameras, booms, microphones, secret service, officials, drivers, mechanics, journalists, going from stop to stop, from one point to another, farcically. In Villepinte, in the expanse of the bus depot, the man I want to see and hear is beyond reach.

Later, at a branch of the Public Transportation Authority, while he expresses his view, after the criminal burning of a Marseille bus, on the absolute nature of the principle of punishment, a cell phone rings (hideous tune):

". . . At seventeen, one can grasp what life is and what death is. Democracy is a system that has to defend itself too . . . You will thank the person who invented this ring tone, because it makes you want to be called. We've got to talk. We have things in common. Anyway, I have completely lost my train of . . ."

Today, I show to Milan and Vera Kundera over lunch two pictures of Nicolas with employees of the company, taken this morning. They are genuinely excited to see him on my cell phone. This is why I like the Kunderas.

Milan, without knowing him, speaks of him and defines him as "a man above and beyond clichés."

At a dinner, the psychoanalyst Jean-Pierre Winter claims that basically he doesn't have a single politician as a patient. They are, in general, men of action, he says, and this would be incompatible.

I transpose it for my own benefit. Forget yesterday.

Two suitors (who will kill me for calling them that) mingle at a party. My name comes up, here is the conversation reported to me by one of them (for my own good):

It's about time something remedied this young parliamentary intern's fascination exerted on our friend by the political world.

About time!

And how do you intend to proceed? I asked.

In Saint-Étienne, just before the meeting, as I arrive by the walkway, I lean out to see the six, seven thousand people who wait for him. Look, he says, you ran for five years in London, two years in New York, but in Saint-Étienne you're nothing!

Coming back. It's nighttime. The men are used to it and get into the cars. Ministers, advisers, members of the cabinet. Barricades, headlights, dark road, airport, checklists, and what for?

In a lounge of the Houari-Boumediene airport, two men, small, are sitting at an angle, on the edge of a corduroy covered couch, legs crossed, one hand resting on top of the other, secretly being swallowed by the yielding cushion, both struggling not to sink in front of the photographers. Mr. Yazid Zerhouni and Mr. Nicolas Sarkozy, Ministers of the Interior of Algeria and France.

"My idea of this country, it comes from books. There are the crowded buses, the walk to the beach where the sun is more yellow, the water more blue, the girls more beautiful. I get here, they tell me I brought the rain and as for the girls, I've got nothing. I am saying this in front of Yasmina, literature is important, it raises your station in life."

. . .

The horde that follows him tramples the tombs, steps over the steles, runs between the crosses, the balustrades, the grilles, the enclosures of chapels, the unending interlaced wrought iron of the Christian cemetery, to extract from him a word, an image.

Later, he will say, I went to meditate at the Martyrs' Monument and at the cemetery of Saint-Eugène.

I am here as if I were in Franche-Comté, says photographer Élodie Grégoire, who has been following him for ten years. On some trips with him, I don't even know where I am or what time it is. My mother is buried in Morocco, continues Rachida Dati,* if I go there alone, my heart misses a beat whenever I leave, I say to myself, I have abandoned her, but if I go with him, I don't feel a thing. Outside, in the garden of the French Residence, he speaks to guests and cameras, his back turned on the night, on the Bay of Algiers, on the illuminated palms of the Martyrs' Monument. The rain has stopped. At the end of his speech, the ambassador's wife thanks God for having held back the sky.

* French politician of Moroccan and Algerian descent. She is the current Minister of Justice and was Sarkozy's spokeswoman during the 2007 presidential election.

.   .   .

Hanging alone on the pale blue wall, in his gilded presidential frame, Abdelaziz Bouteflika watches as we share the barbecued lamb served by his minister. His hair is parted mercilessly down the middle and cascades into gelled crimps of an exceptional reddish brown. The salt-and-pepper mustache is the standard one sported by all government members at the table. The next day, he is there in the flesh and I see for myself that he changed his hairdo. The forehead somehow no longer equipped to maintain the prospect of a part, I can assess the perilous covering of the scalp, with a lateral separation effected from above the right ear all the way across to the left ear, by a brush unflinching and dispassionate.

Color and mustache remained unchanged.

A pedestal table and a bouquet of roses separate them, the two seated in this three-quarter angled position, which, I know, is customary, but nonetheless strange. On respective sides, lined up, silent, five French delegates and four Algerian ministers. No journalists, except for Jean-Pierre Elkabbach,* who is here as a friendly observer.

---

* French journalist who became president of the radio company Europe 1 in 2005.

Nicolas speaks first.

Mr. President, you are looking good.

Yes. I survived a mortal blow, without a single complication. In this métier, one is in need of an iron-clad constitution.

If, by some remote chance, I become president, I will have the pleasure of working many long years with you.

If it is God's will.

So, my future depends on voters and yours on God.

Abdelaziz Bouteflika is serene. He wears a metallic gray tie. He listens impassively and even if he agrees, he doesn't appear to. He seems amused, never on the same page, always one-upping his interlocutor. He calls Nicolas "Dear friend," who, in turn, lavishes him with "Mr. President." Both intent on dispensing these subtle courtesies.

You have pluck and personality. Essential qualities. And you suffer, it is showing in your face. You have some wrinkles. And another five pounds would not hurt you.

The moment of truth is near, Mr. President. But I am not nervous. I'm ready.

You will be taking an exam, dear friend. When you

have worked hard, there is no dishonor in failing. You have no reason to be nervous. If it does not happen this time, it will the next.

It has to happen *now*.

You have an ace up your sleeve, it is age.

There's a lull in the conversation.

Abdelaziz Bouteflika, stone-faced, turns it into a silence. Then, picks up where he left off:

. . . Which should give you all the serenity in the world.

Nicolas remains silent. He lowers his head, stares at the floor, stares at his feet. Then, looks up to meet the gaze of the Algerian president.

Who is waiting.

Flashback to this phrase of Kasparov, *Maybe I can beat Kramnik, but I can't beat the clock*.

In some notes taken in the course of a long interview, certain words stand out.

. . . the globalization that you take as a challenge and not as an ordeal. For us, it is an ordeal. For you, it is a challenge.

You are making your mark but, and I am saying this as a friend, when you have to be firm, say something more. Be firm, but in the same breath, say that you are sensitive to social issues. Say *in the same breath* that social issues do not leave you cold.

I understand.

I come from a generation that wished for the destruction of Israel. We failed. Failed. It is over. I appreciate, dear friend, your position on Israel. But do not forget that the Palestinian people have a right to their own state. And it is a trifle missing in your intonations.

I understand, Mr. President.

Do not be afraid. One should never be afraid. In '99, I did everything I could not to be elected. I said the opposite of what people wanted to hear. Not so important to be unpopular.

I'll remember that, Mr. President.

In the plane that takes us back to France, we speak of the desire for solitude. Which he debunks. He blurts out, I recall, Man was not made to be alone. How selfish, to want to be alone. I don't like myself enough to desire solitude. To be self-reliant, the most egoistic expression . . . Borrowed formulas, so inconsistent with his intelligence. Disregarding the reality that they might express, for him to fall back on these platitudes lays bare an unexpected vulnerability.

He grabs the papers. *Le Figaro, Libération, Le Parisien*. His name and photo on every front page. He barely looks, barely leafs through them. He's suddenly somber. What is it? What remark, what thought, what memory from a trip that went so well? He closes his eyes. Covers them with sunglasses. Michel Gaudin (chief of police) consults his files.

Jean-Pierre Elkabbach and I talk over the engine noise. When he wakes up, no one dares disturb him. In the car that takes us back to Paris, Jean-Pierre cues me in on a detail, this mood swing that separates him from the others and forbids them to break the silence before he does. They've known each other for years. That didn't happen before, he says.

Nathan calls me into his room. I sit on the edge of his bed, in the dark.

Why is it always at night? During the day, I'm caught up in the action of life. Friends, school, I put on my happy face . . . But at night, there is time to be sad.

How many times, these weeks, in public, in the press, or on the airwaves, making rash statements, has G. hyped himself, claiming victory? Never mind the verdict of history. The men that I'm talking about live in a world where words have the weight of helium. Once let loose, they fly away and disappear into the future.

My friend Serge had this thought on politics: "It's a dumb job for smart people."

He is seated on a red plastic chair, next to Jean-Marie Bockel, socialist senator and mayor of Mulhouse, in the Don Bosco community center, for a dialogue with the volunteers of the Coordination Territoriale Drouot and the support group Femmes. The coordinators take turns getting up, chanting, microphone in hand, the mournful music of flattened, functional, wheezing words. What does he think, hearing for the thousandth time in his life, *abdications of parental responsibility, mothers groups, support groups, new forms of solidarity and mobilization, volunteer services, our role in the implementation, partnerships, improve human resources standards* . . . Dead poetry from cold walls, from filing cabinets, dead serious? Where do his thoughts go while he is quietly sitting on the red plastic chair, smiling politely from time to time, God knows why?

An autograph for a husband.
    Your husband, What's his name? . . . Is he handsome?

. . .

What's more surreal than sprinting through the Christmas market in Colmar?

His tired face bares itself.

People say, he hides nothing, he is transparent. He says himself, I have nothing to hide, I show myself as I am. He is looking at the headlines of *L'Équipe,*[*] over the shoulder of Laurent Solly, his chief of staff, head cocked, leaning, like the rest of his body, on the seat back, an attitude of abandon, of exhaustion. From beneath the features, sweetness and something childlike surface. The face bared defies interpretation. I see no transparency, quite the contrary.

"Our compatriots, they have good sense." I make a note of this statement made at EADS, in Élancourt, in the context of the Future of Security conference. It brings back other praises for the sagacity of the people, a memorable one by François Zimeray,[†] a European deputy in 2002: "Jospin[‡] is going to win. Why?

[*] A sports newspaper.

[†] Socialist deputy of the European Parliament.

[‡] Lionel Jospin, politician who was Prime Minister of France from 1997 to 2002. He challenged Chirac for the presidency in 2002 and was defeated in the first round.

Because French people are intelligent." We were a close-knit group. The statement was sincere.

Once you have dedicated your life to the democratic process, maybe you cannot help believing in it a little bit . . .

Back at Élancourt:

I prefer empty auditoriums to shameful auditoriums.

Nice way of defending yourself for being a demagogue. Nevertheless, I doubt that he could sincerely entertain the idea of an empty auditorium.

They are all here or nearly all, the UMP* parliamentarians, in the reception room of the Hôtel Beauvau, standing, listening to him profess his political convictions on the eve of his declaration of candidacy. Lots of familiar faces. Some friends, some enemies.

At one point, he says, I don't usually beg and so it comes as no surprise that nobody gives me anything. A statement I have heard several times in several ways.

The context of these words notwithstanding.

---

* The Union for a Popular Movement (UMP) is the main French center-right political party. Founded in 2002, it has an absolute majority in the National Assembly and the Senate.

.   .   .

"In the presidential election, the one who wins is the one who lets go last scaling Everest. Since '81, all the incumbents have been beaten. I am from the right but I'm not a conservative. The Socialist Party has become an inert party. The greatest risk is not to take one."

Did you like it? he says, spotting me in the hall after his speech.

I'm disoriented by this word "like." What does he mean? The delivery? The tone, the message? And most of all, that he should ask me, me whose gaze sees through any intimation of seduction, scans inconspicuous forms, shadows secret matters.

He moves from clique to clique, clenching men, and that creates little quartets of conspirators, children in the playground, counting down before scattering for a game of cat and mouse.

Campaign meeting in his office.

He is in shirt and tie. The others are in suits.

He is the only one talking for a long time. Making requests, giving instructions. "On every issue, we have to be better. We have to be better positioned, to give better answers . . ." He demands the drafts of his speech for the day after tomorrow (which are not yet ready). "I am going to tell you without arrogance, I am the priority. Without any arrogance. If we can't get my speeches done on time, what's the point? We are now operating at a level where those who can't keep up will have to be canned."

I note the caution with which his staff responds and treats him. Caution, dread. But most dangerous of all for him, the absence of protest.

This weekend, he says, after Marseille, I'm meeting Cécilia and the kids at Disney.

The two of us, face-to-face, across the table, in the Falcon jet going to Lyon. Our first occasion to talk privately again, I believe, since the day we met.

I don't give a damn about Disney. Just to spend time with them, doing things. I love *doing things*. I love running errands, going places. (The day before, to the parliamentarians, he said several times, Inertia is death.)

Later on, about Henri Guaino,* who is involved with the writing of his speeches:

* Speechwriter for Sarkozy, now Special Adviser to the President in the Élysée.

Guaino, he's difficult, but he's a genius. They want to take Guaino away from me. But I need Guaino. I need people like that, who aren't soft. I like freaks, they reassure me.

Reassure you of what?

I don't know . . . That's the thing with anxiety, you don't know where it comes from.

Sometimes, he goes quiet and inspects me. He has gentle and mischievous eyes. I often saw him go quiet and inspect people. In the same fashion. Even people that he would be meeting for the first time.

Much later:

Love is the only thing that matters.

I don't believe you. If your social life stopped tomorrow, you would waste away.

If my family was taken away, even faster.

If they put you with Cécilia and the kids in Maubeuge,* you would throw yourself into the river.

I would be king of Maubeuge in two years flat!

An open space with two trestles, one higher than the other. On the empty town square, just in front of the church, at Neuville-sur-Seine, he is standing, in a navy

---

* Town in northern France, in the department of Nord. Meaning: "Nowheresville."

blue raincoat, which seems to me to flare at the knee.
At his side, ramrod straight in the gray light, bright
scarf, black car coat, the Defense Minister, Michèle
Alliot-Marie. People peer over the security ropes,
with discreet curiosity, unlike the usual crowds. All is
silent. Sporadically, military music and orders called
out in the wind. The coffin arrives, is rested on the
trestles. The French flag unfurled. The cap of the
departed gendarme posed on top. Nobody moves, not
the troops, not the mourning family, freezing under
the blue-and-white striped awning. The Minister
of the Interior says a few words, then steps aside. The
Defense Minister awards two posthumous Medals of
Honor and moves next to the Minister of the Interior.
Commence drumroll. Cease drumroll. Present arms.
At ease.

A prayer for the departed.

Folding of the flag. Funeral march. The gendarmes
leave with the coffin, six of them bearing it. Four others follow, carrying the cushions with the two medals,
the cap, and the folded flag. It took death and solemn
honors to give pause.

A casualty has fabricated time.

He introduces us in the plane. She is different from the
image on television. Softer, more feminine. I find it

amusing to be confronted with this couple of ministers, more or less rivals (they clashed at the Conseil National, and rumor has it that Michèle Alliot-Marie will enter the primary against him). I question her on her experiences at the Defense Department. Before I can finish my sentence, Nicolas turns away and grabs the press strewn about. Face furrowed and already altered by boredom, he plunges into the pages, which he turns at supernatural speed. At the end of it, I see him leafing through some ladies' magazine. We are deep in the account of her helicopter evacuation from a submarine and he doesn't have a single paper left to read. Michèle Alliot-Marie recounts now the night she spent in an Afghani fort (which fascinates me), when, infuriated by his nonexistence, he butts into the conversation to immediately change its direction. We spend the rest of trip on topics, infinitely less exciting for me, such as publishing and our respective royalties . . .

On the tarmac, before getting into his car, he whispers in my ear: "See the difference?"

He is a candidate.

Knowing nothing of political dramatics, I confess to not understanding the importance of this announcement, concerning a man that everyone has considered a candidate from the dawn of time. Samuel Fringant, assistant chief of staff, tells me, In presidential mythology, it's the moment when you cross the Rubicon. There is no going back.

So, this Thursday, November 30, 2006, and according to a terminology constantly revised, "Nicolas Sarkozy is officially in the running for the Élysée."

The very next morning, Laurent Solly raves on the phone, "A little magic is at work, I believe, the transmogrification is complete." Statements as surreal as these spaces in which we dwell.

A few days later, the same Laurent will tell me, Reality doesn't matter. Only perception counts.

Standing in the corridor at France 2, watching him anointed on screen, during the Arlette Chabot* show, he takes his first steps as a candidate.

PIERRE CHARON: What do you think?

Y.R.: Very good.

PIERRE: No, for real?

---

* French journalist and political commentator. She is currently head of the editorial team of France 2, the largest public television network in France, and was one of the moderators of the May 2, 2007, presidential debate between Ségolène Royal and Nicolas Sarkozy.

.   .   .

He is slouched on a low sofa, in the dressing room. He has been talking for three hours. He is calm, seems satisfied. Gathered around him, the intimates, cabinet members. The door opens.

Come in, Arlette, come here, come here!

For a second, I think he is going to ask Arlette Chabot to come sit on his lap. Does she think so too? Miraculously, she succeeds in angling between him and Jeanne-Marie, Cécilia's youngest daughter. They are curiously crammed and she struggles to remain upright.

Hey, he says to her, if you don't smile after a show like that, when are you going to smile?

In Tiercé. A woman in the crowd:

We've been here an hour and there's no way we're gonna see him. All this smoke and mirrors and no sign of the guy!

"I will speak for anyone who thinks he doesn't have energy left in him."

I fancy jotting this down, from his speech in Angers, for no journalist will.

.   .   .

Relax. Yasmina is here. Only because she's kind enough to write about me.

The UMP steering committee at party headquarters. Last to arrive, he sits down next to Jean-Pierre Raffarin,* guest speaker of the day.

A poll is putting us at 51 percent. Ipsos.† It comes out tomorrow. Keep your cool. It doesn't mean a thing. Just as unreliable when it's positive as when it's negative. Getting excited achieves nothing. And What's her name, she's losing it, she's heading for a total meltdown, trying to convince the Iranians that nuclear power is fine for us but not for them.

Jean-Pierre Raffarin takes the stand to go over the rollout of the "Forums de l'Union" that he is coordinating.

The Forums are meant, he says, to show our diversity. We don't want them eclipsed by Nicolas's personality, intelligence, and talent.

What he means is that I should play it modest, calm, you know, be myself.

---

* French conservative politician and senator from Vienne. He was the Prime Minister of France from May 6, 2002, to May 31, 2005, and participated in the construction of the UMP.

† One of the most important polling organizations in France.

He says this while smiling. The Forums get on his nerves, one can see it at a glance.

I am not going to stick to the rule of speaking as much as Michèle Alliot-Marie does. I don't want any constraints on the questions or my response time. But, Jean-Pierre, I assure you, I am no dummy, trust me, I'll be reasonable.

He is not reasonable. He is tense, his mouth is twitching. He detests these Forums designed to contain him, to create an artificial space for anyone else. He vacillates between discipline and devilishness.

Forget Alliot-Marie. She can do whatever she wants. I am going to be relaxed. Maybe I should skip the tie, like on a Saturday? And her, let her do what she wants. (In a stage whisper to Gérard Longuet, let her, let her make her speech, let her hang herself! . . .)

He is not dressed like on a Saturday. Quite the opposite, he couldn't be more formal, white shirt, dark suit, dark tie. He comes out of his dressing room at CNIT and is joined by Michèle Alliot-Marie. On the way to the ring, numbers two and three of the government, flanked by other protagonists of the Forum, are pumped up by a debonair moderator, a hyper, gung ho

Jean-Pierre Raffarin: "Come on, everybody happy! Everybody ready! I only want to see smiles!"

Is he reasonable? In his own way. Michèle Alliot-Marie steps in three times during the two hours of this curious assembly, where "diversity is showing" in vaporous sentences, with no debate, no contradiction, where everyone repeats laboriously what he has hammered ceaselessly, day after day. While the speakers take their turn, he takes a few notes, rubs his chin and his lower lip, plays with his Bic pen, watches them on screen above, then looks right at them, hamming a brand-new half smile, probably projecting his radiant calm (Pierre Lellouche* sends me a text message: "This Forum is tragic!"), presses his hands together, elbows on the table, even has the nerve to bob his head, readjusts his tie, applauds weakly, fidgets with his cell phone, then, suddenly, crosses his arms. He crosses his arms and sits back. An ordinary gesture for anyone else, but which I had never seen before, a rather surprising gesture of physical constraint, of exceptional patience, in the ironical sense of the word,

---

* French conservative politician, member of the UMP. He was also president of NATO Parliamentary Assembly from November 2004 to November 2006.

of disengagement. In his packed dressing room where I slip in before everyone leaves, he hisses to me in passing at the door: "How you doin'? . . . (And adds in a lower voice) What a bunch of bullshit! . . ."

A very high quality debate, he will declare publicly.

"Jacques Chirac's reasoning—he explained it to me as if I were a schoolboy—is that the Russians feel humiliated as a nation . . ."

Breakfast with the experts on Russia and Chechnya. He starts by saying that he will listen before he gives his opinion. Of course, he interrupts throughout.

"Okay. I admit that Russian pride has taken a hit, but is that a reason to keep silent in the face of Putin's transgressions? The Franco-Russian relationship is completely hollow. Just like the Franco-German one. Just like the treaty with Algeria. They're names."

He is the only one fully enjoying what is on the table, croissants, yogurt, coffee; he wants to win this young audience, intellectual, active, concerned, playing the guy who doesn't hold his tongue, his seduction spreading so far that even my steadfast vigilance wavers.

"It has become very important to get rid of the

Quai d'Orsay.* The ambassador to Russia, the last
one, an imbecile, I've seen a few, but this one, I was
embarrassed for him . . . And the ambassador to
Lebanon, another famous knucklehead. It's embarrassing: call him and tell him I said so! I have nothing but
contempt for all of them, they're cowards. And when
you're a coward, you don't think . . . The guy from
Hezbollah likens Israel to the Nazis, the guy is making
a point, and he doesn't get it? What is this, a matter of
translation?"

Sweetness and light. No matter how abrasive Serge
Moati† is, no matter how many times he interrupts,
the tone remains tactful, unflappable, with copious
amounts of *Monsieur Moati* punctuating throughout,
Monsieur Moati, Monsieur Moati, soothing . . . At a
certain point during the show, he is asked to watch a
documentary featuring him twenty years ago, he turns
to the monitor saying, It's always difficult for me to
look at images.

I instantly spot the statement, smuggled in during
this drill. I have written on it before. On the brutal and

* The French Foreign Ministry.
† French artist, journalist, film director, and writer, and formerly a political consultant and public relations manager for François Mitterrand.

noxious advent of images. All our past forms, delusions. Worthless scabs.

The next day, in the foyer of the Ministry, I tell him he was good on the show. He replies, Did you see the ratings? Highest ever on the channel!

Of course. I must have been crazy to think that my praise might have any interest compared to ratings.

Identical error with Fabrice Luchini,* who, one night, at the theater, responded to my appreciation with box office receipts.

Shimon Peres speaks French? He speaks "Peres," retorts David Martinon, the foreign policy adviser. In December 2002, Didier, after an interview with Shimon Peres, told me, During the first seven minutes, I didn't know if my questions were totally destabilizing him or if I was speaking with a Creole leader.

Which is why it would be better, adds David regarding the upcoming visit, if they stick to their mother tongues.

In the hearth, the fire crackles. They are sitting face-to-face, in front of the fireplace. Next to the Israeli Minister, his interpreter. Tall, elegant woman,

* French stage and film actor.

installed with minimum restraint. Shimon Peres is indeed speaking Hebrew, letting, like a goldfish in a bowl, the words escape in minute movements of his lips, body stock-still, face devoid of expression that might animate his famous monotone.

First of all, he mumbles, I wish to express my esteem and the appreciation of my people for your declarations on Iran.

Ahmadinejad should not deny the existence of the Shoah—while he prepares the next one. He should say, I will go down in history having kept an age-old tradition! says Nicolas.

Ken.

Yes! the interpreter blurts out, adding to the exclamation a conspiratorial wink and smirk, which she struggles to suppress.

Is it her intention to translate not just the words but the soul, an irrepressible need to enliven the atmosphere? An emotional involvement, a physical and vocal engagement, so strong that soon she occupies the entire terrain. Shimon Peres has sunk, and in all honesty, so has Nicolas Sarkozy.

Not a single sentence uttered by the two leaders is more luminous in my eyes than the incongruous freedom of this woman.

.   .   .

The UMP. Steering Committee meeting.

Wasn't I good in La Somme? In the flood. Pretty, huh, the rubber boots?

Standing near the door where the executive committee of his party is held, I see the men, some content, some bitter. I see the ones on his side, hesitant or assured, far or close, the ones who are in the group, out front, who directly oppose him, the ones who bustle about or hold their tongues, I see the privileges and the cost of rank.

At the executive committee of his party where I position myself near the door, I see the men.

You have to let me do some poaching, he says to these men who support him. You have to let me surprise. At the risk of throwing a few people for a loop. I'll try to do my best. Things don't always go as planned. I'll try to keep in mind what I am told, but not too much. I need to be able to think on my feet. It's five years I've been knocking myself out on this primary. Did I steal anybody's position? I paid dearly in order to be here, he had said on the occasion of the parliamentarians' reception, I am not here by accident.

And how many times have I heard (always to his own camp): *I have not deprived anyone of his position.*

. . .

Dinner with Jacques Attali.* He knew Sarkozy even before he was mayor of Neuilly. He tells me, He likes the fight, he likes the brawl. He doesn't unify. One must when striving for the presidency. Mitterrand, Chirac unified. Him no.

Incessantly, people speak to me about him. Good or bad. Everybody has a comment on him. He belongs to everyone.

I have the impression that the whole world knows him better than I do.

Five months ahead of the election, I am hearing daily predictions of his defeat.

Ivan, who acknowledges my proximity, but not necessarily my powers of analysis, says to me sadly, He's much brighter than she is, but she's the one with the green thumb.

To the workers of Bogny-sur-Meuse, in the hangar where his voice resonates, he says, *If tomorrow I am President of the Republic.*

---

* French economist and scholar, born in Algeria. From 1981 to 1991, he was a presidential adviser in France's socialist government. In April 1991, he became the first president of the London-based European Bank for Reconstruction and Development.

For the first time, and I don't know why, I experience the fragility, the uncertainty of this ascension.

On the plane to Reims, he rereads his speech with Henri Guaino.

NICOLAS: ... "Economic and social capitulation" ...
I changed it, I put just "social capitulation," I took out "economic" because I remembered that I had been Minister of Finances for two years ... What page are you on? ... On welfare, we should leave "intellectual capitulation," it's better ...

HENRI: No, no, I put back "moral capitulation."

NICOLAS: "Moral," you think? ... "I'm not going to cry with you because, here, nobody ever cries" ... I changed it to: "I'm not going to cry with you because true pain, one keeps to oneself" ... *One keeps to oneself,* you see ... That's it. I did well, huh?

Guaino acquiesces.

Intermittently, as he is answering calmly to students of the agricultural college of Rethel, there is a flapping, as if shaken by violent gusts, of the panel of tablecloth that covers his table down to the floor. Believing himself protected by the fabric, he can praise the future of biofuels while kicking into the emptiness.

The "fettling presses" drive holes. With a weighty strike, a heavy noise, they fall on the molten steel. What is heard and which deafens are the presses landing on the red rods. An enormous arm deposits the incandescent cast iron, the press drives a hole, another seizes the holed object and poses it delicately on the conveyor. After each movement, the robots that pose and deposit, dressed in anoraks made of pleated material, pause a half second to contemplate the ultimate purpose of the gesture. The men in blue follow us, glove in hand. We walk around in their cavern as if in another country. Accompanying the minister in mid-campaign, to breathe the air of the forges and contemplate the fate of the burning-hot parts.

In the lobby of the hotel, before the meeting at Charleville-Mézières, he snatches *Le Figaro* from my lap, visibly drawn to an article.

On the front page, Ahmadinejad's electoral setback and then diverse subheads, one on his own appearance.

At the bottom of the page, on the right, an ad.

After several seconds of concentration, he says, This Rolex . . . rocks!

. . .

End of December. Ten at night. After the long day in the Ardennes.

He hangs out with us in the courtyard of the Hotel Beauvau. Customarily, he gets out of the car and disappears into the door leading to his office or his living quarters. Tonight, he lingers a little longer; again he asks if the day went well. He is tired. He wears his blue cashmere coat open at the top. No tie, shirt unbuttoned. Slovenly for him and slightly strange in the cold of winter.

We hug. We part.

In the car that drives me back, I am amazed to see him still in the doorway, alone, facing the night, his bare neck peeking out from the full coat, waving his goodbyes.

"To be adult is to be alone."

Recurring thought of this, written by Jean Rostand.*

To the one-day-old baby girl, I had whispered, You don't belong to me, you're going to grow up and I will teach you how to be alone.

* French biologist and philosopher.

Not long ago, Nicolas told me: "I know how to be solitary when I have to make decisions. That's it."

They play big. That's what moves me. They play big. They are both the player and the bet. They put themselves on the table. It's not their life they are putting on the line, but, more gravely, their notion of it.

In a film on Jacques Chirac by Patrick Rotman, one sees him in 1980, when he is only twenty-five and looking fourteen, the tie, the blow-dried hairstyle of the right-wing student.

"At the time, you're young, he says in a more recent interview from the same film, you're pretty passionate, and politics fulfills your every expectation, emotions, vibrations, passion sometimes."

He says nothing of the kind on his life today. Quite the contrary.

This morning, a phrase of Daniel de Crozefon: "Far away, emotion thrills me. Close up, it assaults me."

He believes in supernatural intervention. When people say to him, I will pray for you, he earnestly encourages them. He told me that, in Africa, a gray bull was sacrificed for his sake. You believe in that stuff? I asked. In my situation I'm ready to believe in anything.

This morning in *Libération,* an astrologer and two psychics predict his defeat. He is vacationing abroad. I hope he will not read the paper.

Strange afternoon spent at Agence Gamma looking at photos by Élodie Grégoire. I confine myself to the last two years, being short on time (and exhausted).

First off the heap, all those in which he wears a costume. He is a nurse, he is a cheesemonger, he is an iron founder, he is a chemical engineer, he is an African in a boubou . . . Not one outfit is truly taken on, not one jells, always an item amiss, a bonnet, a hard hat, a mobcap, an apron untied or sideways, his tailored suit mutinies under a tunic. He can never quite pull off these disguises. I set aside other pictures, more predictable. Hand gestures, finger movements, postures that I am getting to know well, the same over and over. Just before a public appearance, standing, hands clasped, legs slightly apart, eyes down, staring at the ground. If the face were hidden, I could still identify him immediately.

Some of them show him walking around alone

(with two bodyguards not visible) in Paris. In February 2006. He has stopped to speak with a rare-stamps seller. They are both laughing. He wears a dark coat and a royal blue scarf. He laughs with the seller, his hands clamped behind his back. He is neither rushed nor trying to impress. The seller is older, well covered from the cold, coolly seated in his stand. He does not seem to be intimidated. This absolutely pedestrian photo is the most extraordinary of all (Élodie will tell me later, he has referred to it many times, like it was an event, to that improvised stroll in the streets, after an official photo shoot).

From this long parade of images on the screen remain above all infinite nonplaces, halls, stages, airplane steps, cement barriers, official banquettes with interchangeable luminaries, sparse trees behind black cars most often masking hideous housing projects, and in these abiding backdrops, repeating the same efforts, the same man, at the center of it all, come what may.

"For this year's final pressing-of-the-flesh, Nicolas Sarkozy chose the Christmas market in Orléans . . ." one reads in the paper. An agitated pressing-of-the-flesh full of tension, on one side, people screaming Sarko President, on the other, Sarko Everywhere Justice Nowhere, among other invectives. They are identical, victims of a vociferating hysteria, of an identical dissolution of the individual being into the throng.

In Marseille today, a woman perched on a traffic light: "What are you doing here, motherfucker? Get the fuck out of here!"

He looks up at her. Then continues on, still smiling, cutting through the surge.

So often, I have seen him grab papers, glance without reading, turn the pages lickety-split. It took a long time to understand what I was seeing, the mind contents itself with preconceived notions, they are tough-skinned, bulletproof . . . One day, suddenly, something hit me and I said, Do you protect yourself? I have no choice, was his response.

Later, when he exits the police precinct of Noailles, he is whistled at and booed by a spontaneous assemblage.

A journalist asks him, on the flight back, to interpret the violent reactions he arouses; he evades the question and hides behind a vague sociological speech. I am astonished because it is not his habit to dodge or skirt.

. . .

I happen to be alone with him in his drawing room. I am curious to know what he registers of this partly hostile day. Behind us, the dining table is prettily set for Christmas Eve dinner. I have asked if I may watch with him the president's final season's greetings. I am not quite sure that he would have watched it had I not requested it. I really don't know. He is wearing a white shirt and a black velvet jacket. No tie. He does not know how to turn on the television; he picks up the phone several times to ask, The greetings are on at what time?

Republican music.

He sits down with an orange juice.

Jacques Chirac appears. His eyes are bulging and his complexion has a deathly pallor. Nicolas says, Hou là là! Later, he will say, I don't know if it's the television or him . . . (it is the television).

We are listening in silence. I will pass on the head nodding and the distinctive leg movements (mild to moderate).

He reacts to nothing, or nearly nothing. I believe neither the indifference nor the detachment. He is probably not expecting anything from this final address, but I have to take into account the influence of my presence and that, for once, I have obliged him to "land." Cécilia arrives. Sits. Stands up, busies herself with the fire, with the lighting, with the television cord, consults her BlackBerry. Finally, undertakes watching.

The president disappears. Nicolas cuts the sound off and refuses to listen to the rest of the news. His comments: "Predictable and old-fashioned. No perspective. If I were he, I would have said, Here, I have served you for twelve years, a new era is coming . . ." But, a few minutes later, we have moved on to something else; he adds, vivaciously: "Still, I see energy in the old lion."

He picked it up himself. Cécilia's Christmas present, he says.

A large black-and-white photograph, framed, signed Harcourt, of his three sons, the two older flanking the youngest.

It was Cécilia's idea, it was she who had the idea. She surprised me. It's a Christmas present from her. It's no small thing, getting these three together in one place! She gave me a great gift, Cécilia. It's not the photograph that he is showing me. What he is showing me is Cécilia's gesture. And it's Cécilia's gesture that he props on the arms of a chair.

.   .   .

At midnight, we embrace each other. We are in the year 2007. But we embrace each other as if it were any other year. It is obvious he wants it that way.

We part in the foyer of Beauvau. Smiling, he goes into the garden with Big, a Chihuahua, of which he is ashamed.

One day, G. said to me, I am eternal.

An irritating and defining remark.

This morning, New Year's Day, as I find the words G. sent me during the night, I have proof he thinks himself eternal. He does not see death coming. He has a genius for self-distraction. How does he do it?

Contrary to my initial prejudice, I am not sure Nicolas Sarkozy is blessed with this enviable frivolity when faced with the passage of time.

Lunch with Jean-Michel Goudard.

He has caught a cold running in the woods. We discuss his jogging schedule. He confesses a lack of consistency recently. "But I'm training, in order to surprise Nicolas. Before, I blinded him, but now he's better, he runs for an hour. I can't run for an hour at his pace. But I'm back in training. What I would like, would be to trail him—anyway, Nicolas couldn't stand to see me out front—and, at the very end, to slam him. Can you see it, I come around the side, very cool, at the last minute, to show him that I have some in reserve. And finally, I let him finish first, just to make him happy."

Jean-Michel Goudard is sixty-eight years old.

So many days left. So many weeks. So many months. Counted and recounted, for no reason, the time that lies between us and May 6. Depending on the mood, he says, it's long or it's short.

Campaign meeting. First of the year.

In front of the fireplace, in his office, sitting in a semicircle, fifteen people or so. Members of his team and prominent members of society. It seems to me there are too many people, the essential is diluted.

He, sitting in his usual place, next to the fire, legs quivering, cigar.

"These meetings with politicians are mostly held to keep them happy, not to listen to their advice. So, here's the way I see the campaign. On one side, an executive committee, you. On the other, a tight political team whose mission is to make them happy."

Ajaccio.

The socioprofessional representatives are sitting

gloomily around tables set for lunch. I see him in profile, standing in front of the microphone. I see the
crunched neck, the buffalo hump, sort of, the jacket
with flaps floating; if the belly expanded, I say to
myself, and if the hair whitened, he would quickly
have the dull aspect of gasping political animals; it
doesn't take much, I say to myself, to fall into that
look, into the danger that awaits, if life does not fulfill
its promises, and it is not just a defeat for the body.

One hour later, at the Prefecture, during a restricted
committee meeting on national security, he speaks to
the cops, like a cop. Sitting around a square table with
various officials, superintendents, investigators, head
of RG, head of CRS, he is one of them.

Keep at it. Keep at it. I'm confident. Don't let them
breathe. Hunt them down. I'm sick of these funerals
with fifty Mafia guys showing up.

Hoarse voice, sidelong glance. Robert Stack in *The
Untouchables*.

No connection between the Mafia and the elected
representatives?

Some issues for local power and public works at
stake.

He nods. A man on the ground. That he is too. And
a man of few words.

DAWN, DUSK OR NIGHT

Then, lowering his voice.

Do not hesitate. I don't have friends. In any case, I don't want friends who would be caught red-handed in this thing. Go ahead.

"You can see him better on TV," says a local. He is standing not so far from her, yet unseen at less than three meters, surrounded by his usual swarm of microphones and cameras. Having arrived by helicopter in Sainte-Lucie-de-Tallano, we are walking through the village toward the local hostel, passing an ancient olive press that's been restored. A loudspeaker hooked up outside relays the voices of those people speaking in a little hall on this stop. Over a light wind and the babbling of a stream. The words waft, to die away beyond the road in the setting sun of winter: federal-funding project, territorial organization, microregional development, rurality . . . He has not seen a thing. He has not seen the pines, the bare cherry trees flanking the Genoese houses, the smoking chimneys. He has not seen a thing except for this black cloud staying ahead of him, he has moved on like on any other sidewalk, speaking to journalists, elected officials, a few lucky bystanders. He has not tried to look, not once has he pulled aside the infernal curtain, come closer to the low wall that overlooks the jagged beauty. Not once has he wished to stop. Only for a few seconds to look at the high houses and imagine who lives here, at the austere stones dominating the ravines as far as the eye can see. He has not seen, clinging to the steep slopes, the forests of evergreens, oaks, olive trees, chestnut trees, turning orange in the dying day. He has not seen a thing.

Later, in the plane back to Paris, I hear him say: "That village, it's gorgeous."

I find in my notebooks this remark uttered during another appearance. "I can only love a landscape if I'm in it with someone I love." A formula so vain. Like all those in which he brandishes the banner of love. And so he keeps at his disposal a set of professed beliefs in a box, reflections of reflections, he might give credence to, in the end.

Still in the plane coming back from Corsica, he says to Charles Jaigu from *Le Figaro* and Philippe Rider from *Le Monde:* "I continue to be an inexhaustible source for your shitty articles!" We note it, all three of us, and they admit with regret that only I will be able to use this outburst.

. . .

They are in the little study in his private apartments, preparing the speech for the nomination.

Outside, it is dark.

He, sitting on the sofa, smoking a cigar, checked shirt and flannel trousers. Henri Guaino is in an armchair, on the other side of the curiously serpentine coffee table.

HENRI (putting pages in order): . . . I'm not too happy with the ecological proposals, not a single one hits home.

NICOLAS: We put on polluters what we put on workers . . . Hey, not bad! Not bad at all! Never said it that way before! I am not afraid to use the word "worker"!

HENRI: Yeah, not bad.

NICOLAS: One thing I have yet to say, and fuck, there is so much to say about it, it's *a Republic, above and beyond reproach*. Go for broke on that.

HENRI: Okay.

NICOLAS: We also have to say: I ask my friends to let me be.

HENRI: That's not just good, it's very good! Very good!!

They beam at each other. In my notebook, I wrote and circled, "Two sentimental souls."

NICOLAS (on a high, on his feet, improvising words that Henri jots down, teeth bared): . . . France shouldn't just be nostalgia. Bowing and scraping to the past should not obscure the future . . . Great nations hampered by a long history will forget the future . . . China is wedded to the future! . . . You see, Henri, my friend? (He gives him a high five.) This could be the most important speech of my life, I need you, not because I love you, but because we're on the same wavelength!

He is pacing, cigar in hand. Behind him, in the bookcase, a large blue moiré volume facing us: *Charles de Gaulle—Speeches*. He opens the window. The wet wind of the night blows into the room, the fire flares in the hearth.

HENRI: To me, the main idea . . . is work.

NICOLAS: Okay, Okay! Okay! The running thread is work! For me, there are two ideas, France is not finished, and work.

(I think again of Fabrice's phone call, "Royal is proposing virtual reality. That's better than him, tirelessly

proposing we get up early in the morning. Who wants
to get up early in the morning?")

   HENRI: The thing to do on that day is to watch not
               for the applause, but for the silence, the
               silence in the room.

NICOLAS: But wait, wait! . . .

   Impatient gestures of the hand, the head, that con-
vey, I know, I know before you, better than you,
which silence you mean! . . . And he launches, in a low
voice, ardent, for the two of us, but facing fifty thousand people, into a tribute to Georges Mandel.*

*The childhood of a leader, The hundred days that will change
his life, The true nature of Nicolas, What nobody's ever told
you about Sarkozy, Élysée-moi, Dashing Sarkozy . . .* He is
on the cover of every weekly, on the front page of all
the dailies, entire pages on his strengths, his weak-
nesses, his feelings, his wives, his secrets, his ambi-
tions, his image, his ego, his desires . . . Since the
beginning of this year, no less than four or five books

---

* French politican, journalist, and Resistance leader, outspoken opponent
of Nazism and fascism, murdered in 1944 in retaliation for the assassina-
tion of the Vichy Minister of Propaganda, Philippe Henriot, by members of the Maquis.

are devoted to him, adding to dozens of others already published, hagiographies, comics, lampoons . . .

And this astounding remark of Michael Darmon,[*] author of one of the most recent books: "People don't know him. People don't know who he is." In the revolving door of Hôtel Lutétia.

"The more he is in the light," observes also my friend François, "the more he becomes opaque."

"And Catherine Nay's[†] book, is it any good?"

Porte de Versailles. Saturday night, January 13. Eve of his acceptance speech.

In a room that will temporarily serve as his dressing room the next day, he is sitting in a black leather armchair. Around him, Brice Hortefeux,[‡] Pierre Charon, Patrick Devedjian,[§] Claude

---

[*] French political journalist for France 2, known for his reporting on *Envoyé Spécial,* also author of *La Vraie Nature de Nicolas Sarkozy.*

[†] French political journalist who became adviser to the president of Europe 1, Jean-Pierre Elkabbach, in 2005.

[‡] French politician and Minister of Immigration, Integration, National Identity, and Cooperative Development, member of the UMP.

[§] French politician who is currently president of the General Council of Hauts-de-Seine, the richest department in France. He was also named executive secretary-general of the UMP and is now sharing the direction of the UMP with Jean-Pierre Raffarin.

Guéant,* Laurent Solly, Frédéric Lefebvre,† Franck Louvrier,‡ David Martinon.§

"And what else, not too much bullshit?"

He is being reassured. Made to admit that he is sultry, unshaven on the cover of *L'Express,* with Cécilia. "I should let my beard grow then?"

As is his habit, clearly, he has read almost nothing. I write almost because he is aware that *Le Parisien* managed to get his first wife to talk. (*"When we were together, Nicolas and I were practicing Catholics. I hope for his sake that he still believes in God and finds peace."*)

To go and interrogate Marie! Can you imagine? . . . And her, you'd think she would have called me before saying I was close to God when I was young!

You were close to God when you were young?

Watch your mouth, Yasmina . . .!

A cell phone rings. His eldest son. Dulcet tones, diminutives, words sugary sweet, promises to hurry

---

* French civil servant, President Sarkozy's secretary-general—an office similar to chief of staff.

† Former adviser of the regional council of Île-de-France, currently deputy of the tenth constituency of Hauts-de-Seine.

‡ Communications adviser for Sarkozy since 1997.

§ Member of Sarkozy's inner circle during the campaign.

home after the meeting, kisses, tenderness with such *alacrity* exchanged in undertones.

"You know what's the worst, is the advice. Anyway, I don't listen to them. They brutally tell you it's too early, and then, no less brutally, they tell you it's too late. The advice always adds up to: not right now."

Suddenly, he is cheerful, relaxed. A little bit for my benefit, I imagine without pretension, being the new arrival, and since everybody knows the stories, he starts to recount the beginnings as mayor of Neuilly with Brice, the pranks, their trip to the United States. "I was twenty-eight, you were twenty-five . . . We only clashed once in thirty years. He knew two girls, he told me, one is for me, the other one you don't stand a chance, in return for which I was the one who had to pay for dinner! . . ."

He has some time. He has nothing left to do here, but he is lingering. He is lingering to speak, to laugh with his friends (I write "friends," but I should say "entourage," I am not sure of the word "friend," even for those who avail themselves of this abusive term; I write "friends" in an outburst of empathy because I don't think I ever observed such abandoned levity).

"So here we are, twenty-five years later . . . It was more fun then." He says that, smiling, with a certain sweetness. Joy, insolence, desire to eat the world and a whole life to do it . . . Tomorrow, at the podium, in front of thousands of people, he will say, France, my country, the cathedrals, he will say Valmy, Jaurès,* and Brother Christian. But at this moment, he says: "Now, you are the ones jumping the girls." He is not in a rush. He wants to laugh with his staff and his "friends." He is still sitting, without worry, in the dim light of the makeshift decor.

In the car that takes us back, Laurent and Pierre, who have known a lot of the same moments, inform me of their nostalgia.

An hour earlier, while everybody hastened the last preparations, I saw him, hands in his coat pockets, going back down the large white stairs, all alone. At mid-level, he stopped. He contemplated the immense space of the Parc des Expositions, the rows of empty seats in front, on the sides, at the back. He turned to face the screen where a virtual bird was flying over a green vale.

Once at the bottom, he took Jean-Michel aside: At

---

* French socialist leader, one of the first social democrats, founded *L'Humanité* and was assassinated in 1914.

the end, tomorrow, I don't want to be alone. Understand me . . . I will have spoken for an hour, fine but . . . I shouldn't be alone . . .

Who do you want to be with? Politicos?

I don't want to be alone . . . Make the whole front row come up. I want us all to go out together. I don't want to go out alone.

Sunday, January 14.

Backstage, while other speakers are warming up the audience, conversation with Henri Guaino, whom I have not seen since the first working session. He seems satisfied with the speech but deplores a last-minute change. (Henri would not be Henri without something to deplore). What Henri deplores is the striking-out of the word "crossbreeding." After having defended it ardently, with brilliant arguments, says Henri speaking of Nicolas, he ended by coming round to X and Y's opinion, who considered the term dangerous. Once we begin to fear words, we are slipping down the fatal slope of defeat! he adds in this vehement and irritated tone, which is also part of his charm. Did you tell him? I asked. I passed him a few lines, basically stating, You never win by not being yourself.

Consequently, an hour later, in the course of the nomination speech, Henri Guaino will have the joy of hearing not once, but twice, the word "crossbreeding."

Two photographs. In two opposing dailies. Taken the day after his nomination, at the top of the Mont-Saint-Michel abbey. Two photographs taken at the same time, I find them in the press like everybody else.

Nicolas, black turtleneck and coat, in the solitude of a medieval corbel, face chiseled against a pale sky, meditating over the bay.

A ferocious herd bearing microphones and cameras, contained behind a barrier, separated by five meters of artificial emptiness from a minuscule Nicolas, astray, on the right-hand side of the photo, oddly isolated in the middle of a stony cornice.

By the middle of the meeting, his mood softened. Why? I couldn't say. It often occurs, he can be tense when he arrives, preoccupied, and suddenly lightens up.

For Berlin, I want to go with Juppé. Beautiful idea, huh? . . . I'm going to spend a hell of a day with Juppé and Merkel . . . But then! . . . I don't want to do Madrid right after, I don't want to seem like Speedy Gonzales.

If you go to Madrid, visit a museum, suggests Georges-Marc Benamou.*

Thank you. The stupid bastard says thank you.

No matter how hard the little assembly laughs, his sarcasm doesn't appease his vanity, and he immediately embarks on a dissertation, several minutes long, about Picasso, *Guernica,* the Reina Sofia, Velázquez, *Las Meninas,* noble topics without the slightest connection to the campaign.

Plateau of Saclay. He is sitting at a table with researchers and university presidents. Behind him, a poster, "Nanosciences at Soleil." It would be an understatement to say that this crowd is not in his corner. On one side, the noble, the ivory tower, the brainpower; on the other, the mongrel, the politician. They make certain that he feels it.

A researcher has to be subversive, if you'll pardon my saying so, Mr. Minister.

What gives you the right to say that I'm not subversive? Old friend, you don't get the papers in Saclay?

The scientists smile politely.

. . .

* French journalist, born in Algeria, who is the cultural and audiovisual adviser to Sarkozy.

He asks the question: "Who manages all of this? Who decides?"

The president of CNRS* launches into a brief demonstration, the discreet haughtiness of which culminates in: "Decides what? Your question does not make any sense." Smiling, he regards her, speechless, as if dazzled by the audacity. Somebody else takes over. He is genuinely interested. Then:

"Excuse me, it seems silly . . . But it's on purpose . . . No, but . . . (he takes the arm of the person nearest him) . . . No, but . . . Huh, I . . . I don't want . . . (he smiles, feigning shyness) . . . I don't want to . . . I was going to say militarize, in front of the general . . . (the general being the head of École Polytechnique) . . . I have a feeling everybody's sensitive, so I'm walking on eggshells here! . . . Pardon me if I go back to it . . . Deciding what? A strategy. It's not about right or left, it's a matter of coherence . . . Huh . . . How best to utilize the resources that we are going to set aside for French research. I'm not trying to be pushy . . . But still . . . In order to put a strategy in place, we need a *direction*.

How many times these snippets of words, these falsely aborted sentences, these coy hesitations! The

* Largest governmental research organization in France.

greatest charm offensive, in the original meaning of the word, a bewitching, beguiling clumsiness that propagates an idea.

To go to the Aveyron, he sports a pink shirt and black tie. I point out to him that he has renounced the polka-dot tie. Yeah, what do you think? I say I am not against this combination, but Élodie disagrees. Anyway, I don't give a damn, he says, I don't give a damn what you think, I belong to my public. Like Monty (the sixties teen idol).

He saw at home, on his new television, *The Silence of the Lambs,* he found the movie terrific and Jodie Foster too, he repeats over and over that Jodie Foster is terrific, and the wide screen is terrific too, he says that he never intended to see *The Silence of the Lambs,* but he didn't find the movie too disturbing in the end, he says they put the little one to bed and he watched the movie with Cécilia and Jeanne-Marie, he says, Anthony Hopkins is terrific too, he says he never had a country house but he wouldn't mind now, to give the kids roots, dogs, a little horse for Louis, a motorcycle, he comments on *L'Équipe* with the journalists on board, latest news on OM, he says, Santoro, he's still on top of it, he is so used to being the one who speaks and the one who is listened to, he alone is entitled to divulge his ordinary life without being interrupted, without anyone looking bored, it doesn't occur to him that his ordinary is just as ordinary as it is for the next man.

The confidential trip to the women's prison in Rennes starts with the Family Visit Facility. A ground-floor one-bedroom, next to the prison, a kind of miniature apartment, shrunk down to the essentials, with a sliding window open to a patch of lawn, a wall, and a fence of iron. The women who have access to these facilities are permitted to see their husband, their children, during forty-eight hours, once a quarter. "Time flies for them," says the assistant warden, "every semester, bam, they apply, they're happy, time flies for them." A perspective confirmed by a prisoner to the Minister: "The goodbyes are heartbreaking, yes. At least the first few times. But we know we're going to get another appointment in three months." Another appointment in that utilitarian space, dropped somewhere on earth, just as it could have been dropped anywhere else, the three-seat sofa, the few chairs, the TV, the bedroom that cannot contain anything save the solitude of a large bed. Another appointment to see a child do his homework on an institutional table, to be in a man's arms for two days, in fugitive arms, and in no-man's-land.

I look at Nicolas Sarkozy, sitting, listening to the girls, his back to the window. What is he thinking, he who stirs up life incessantly? What does he think of the time that flies when the prospect of being loved a little, caressed a little, for two days, where no one lives, so compels?

In the prison chapel, upon leaving, I hear this exchange between Sister Anne and him.

Life is heavy.

Yes.

Not just in jail, Sister. Life is heavy.

With utter earnestness, he comments, right outside the penitentiary, for the local press, on the passing of Abbé Pierre,* which occurred overnight, and with the same grave expression, with the same tone of condolence, on the comforting non-candidacy of Nicolas Hulot . . .

·   ·   ·

* French Catholic priest, born Henri-Antoine Grouès, member of the Resistance during World War II, and deputy of the Popular Republican Movement (MRP). In 1949 he founded the Emmaus movement, which has the goal of helping poor and homeless people and refugees.

On the plane.

Lucky, Abbé Pierre didn't die on Sunday, the fourteenth . . .

Chirac called to tell me that he is confident. (Stricken face.) I said, I don't believe you. You'll see, you'll see. You've been calling for the last six months to tell me that you were concerned. I didn't believe you then and I don't believe you now. (In a variety of tones). I am confident . . . I am confident . . . I am confident, he said to me!

Reread this passage of Louis-René des Forêts,[*] *It's likely that existence, even for those who feign to stride through life, is no more than a labyrinth in which each of us wheels around seeking an exit nowhere to be found . . .*

A pause before the meeting, in the Saint-Quentin town hall. In the Marriage Hall's wood-paneled antechamber, he whispers to Henri Guaino:

Henri, for my speech on the fifteenth, to the kids, I want to be completely different, I want to start say-

[*] French writer, died in 2000, who participated in the French Resistance during World War II and created an organization to oppose the Algerian War in 1954.

ing that I am to be the president of the twenty-first century . . .

I laugh.

You're laughing? Fuck you. Do you understand what that means?

Later, when he catches me by myself:

Yasmina Reza, you're going to tell me why president of the twenty-first century is so funny?

Marvelous Henri, front row center, smiling, prompting, murmuring the words as they come . . . *Jaurès* . . . *Blum* . . . *Clemenceau* . . . murmuring *there are no opposite camps* (when France is at stake) . . . the Left knows *nothing* . . . craning his neck, arms crossed, mouth half open, murmuring when he hits the sentence about *Général de Gaulle* . . . whispering *There was only one* (France) . . . a little boy, with salt-and-pepper hair, precisely parted, listening to the schoolteacher read his essay to the class.

"The beauty of seeing you with my eyes!" a woman with a foreign accent says, as Nicolas is passing by, who tends her husband lying on a stretcher. He smiles. He is somewhere else. Strange night visit at the Medical Center René-Dubos in Pontoise. A silent stroll around the wards that he has probably seen a hundred times, slipping into tiny glass offices to shake hands and hear about how hard life is, wandering among the computers of the control room of SAMU, listening indifferently to reports ("It was just screams; the reason of the call is that he's dead. Except that he was breathing."). He walks down the corridors, gloomily lit, limping a bit, he jokes with the Health Minister and a girl from AFP, the only journalist present. In a black turtleneck and herringbone jacket, the head of security guiding us is twenty meters ahead; he walks down the corridors, cell phone clutched in hand, hobbling, tapping his fingers along the wall. He gives the impression of not caring where he's going.

While Nicolas Sarkozy and Tony Blair have a tête-à-tête, I have lunch with Jonathan Powell, his chief of staff, David Hill, his spokesman, and Michel Barnier.*

After coffee, Nicolas appears with Tony Blair. Nicolas introduces me as a genius writer and Tony replies politely that he has heard through the grapevine of my London successes. (I find myself trans-

---

* Conservative French politician who was elected vice president of the European People's Party in March 2006 and became Minister of Agriculture in June 2007.

ported to twenty years ago on rue de Rennes with my father introducing me to Raymond Barre, and I cannot remember a word of English).

I am the first one to exit 10 Downing Street to face a crowd of journalists on the other side of the pavement (I smile modestly because at this instant it is I who lunched tête-à-tête with the English prime minister).

In the vestibule:

Okay, no spies? We made a decision, Tony and I, we're going to conquer Europe!

In the meantime, they both pose gaily in the front of the door. A rare image, I am told, reserved according to protocol to personalities of equal rank.

In Job Center Plus (a combination of Unemployment and Welfare), a young man calls out: "Hey, you're looking for a job?"

"Perhaps," he replies.

Visit to the Churchill Museum. A faster visit to the premises is *literally* impossible.

Completely depressive, this poor Churchill, he'll say. He'll say it again, on the train to Montceau-les-Mines, as I reproach him for this headlong charge of the "War rooms." You're not sensitive to Churchill, I say. No. I'm disheartened by this answer. Even if you cycle in skintight shorts and you jog, even if you are the most temperate of men and if you never played at war games, how can you not be sensitive to Churchill? I keep my mouth shut because the head of Alstom* and the UMP treasurer are here, but how could you not adore Churchill, had you seen him as I have, in an archive film, hurtling down a child's slide into a swimming pool, body of a walrus, insane paunch, bellowing laughter, the magnifico, the hero, the wino, belly-flopping vertigo, into the water . . . peals of laughter!

On his physical training (and mental), Didier says to me, Deep down he lacks street smarts and the anarchist streak, he is American in the worst sense of the word.

We are waiting for Marc Lévy,† having tea in the lounge of the Savoy. Amicable tone and that touch of

---

* Large French multinational conglomerate whose businesses are power generation, railway signaling, and manufacturing trains (for example, the TGV and Eurostar as well as Citadis trams) and the world's largest ships (for example, the *Normandie* and the *Queen Mary 2*).

† French writer whose novel *Et si c'était vrai* . . . was adapted for the screen in 2005 with the title *Just like Heaven*.

impatience in it, a discreet allusion that *I am a snob,* is only natural. "I'm sorry, but a guy who sells millions of copies, I'm interested. If I don't read Marc Lévy, if I don't watch the Tour de France, I might as well do another job. Watch out, he's coming."

A conversation between two authors:

NICOLAS SARKOZY : My greatest goal was to be in Palavas-les-Flots, between the buoys and the guys from the press.

MARC LÉVY : I was there myself.

NICOLAS SARKOZY : I know. Always ahead of me in sales. My daughter says to tell you that she loves you. She is a huge fan. That's why, I said to myself, I'm going to beat him. But you're always ahead.

MARC LÉVY : You should be in paperback. Your book was fantastic, you should be reaching a whole new public, young.

NICOLAS SARKOZY : If you could sign an autograph for Jeanne; she would be so . . . Don't you have a piece of paper, Yasmina, if I'm going to be tacky, I might as well go all the way!

He is truly one of your characters, says a friend to whom I just read a few passages of this text.

He says, The day before yesterday, I was in a factory, I got up on a crate and I made a little speech. Before him, elegant suits, loving looks, and glasses in hand, the sponsors.

The little speech up on a crate, he can't stop telling that story. Every week, I go to factories, I get up on a crate and I talk. The little speech on the crate, in the workshop among milling machinists and fitters, words that he loves to reel off, it's his pride and joy.

Same audience.

Madame Royal, is she helping or hurting? Who knows? Who knows if being a zero hurts you in France?

There is a riot to get into the hall at Old Billingsgate Market, venue for his address to the French of London. After entering the building, with some difficulty, I join him in his dressing room, as he is being made up. I say, It's worse than Mick Jagger. He is delighted by

my comparison. He'll say, on the way back, to
François Fillon,* they hadn't seen anything like that
since the Beatles!

In the plane, he consents to say a few words into the
camera, for the reporters of *Envoyé Spécial.*† A man sits
on the side, with an enormous contraption, Soviet-
looking, right out of a Tintin comic book. An
extremely discreet microphone from French Public
Television! says Nicolas. (On the broadcast that I will
watch on France 2, this interview will be particularly
inaudible.)

He is the last speaker at the Sustainable Development
Forum organized by Nicolas Hulot. Decent speech,
that he tries to render his own, with little success. (The
eco niche, you haven't rehearsed that one very much,
remarked Jaigu in Aveyron. Niche, the dumbest word
on earth, the green niche, it truly bugs the shit out of
me.) It is not like him, this inevitable genuflection, to
which his opponents have docilely lent themselves, fifteen minutes at a time, right before him. And nothing

---

* Current Prime Minister of France, having been appointed to that office
  by President Sarkozy on May 17, 2007.

† Weekly newsmagazine on France 2.

is working. Not even the elevator in Quai Branly, which refuses to transport us, then starts moving again once we get out of it.

At the end of the "allotted" fifteen minutes, a moderator, onstage, signals him that his time is up. As he wraps up, we hear, in the hall, mechanical voices that nothing will deter, *time is up, time is up,* injunctions bearing the stamp of righteousness, making defenders of this essential issue so contemptible. Without wavering, he concludes.

Rungis, Pavillon de la Marée, five in the morning, everyone has put on a white cotton coat, he is wearing . . . a white ski jacket.

You figured out a way to be elegant.

Do I look ridiculous?

Pavillon de la Triperie, in a café.

A waitress:

Did he kiss you? Me too! As a matter of fact, he's a handsome man, I could see him as president.

He takes us aside for two seconds, Élodie and me, as he knows how to do, one under each arm:

I'm a huge hit with the girls!

In front of a vat of calves' feet, Élodie says to me, He should always wear a turtleneck. We're going to tell him.

. . .

They want to see him, touch him, kiss him. He disappears amid crates of endives, crates of lychees, pineapples, tomatoes.—You're going to suffocate him, guys! Hey! He's still a baby!

You're superconfident?

If I was superconfident, I wouldn't be getting up at four a.m. I am only saying that February 1, I'm where I want to be. I'm psychologically prepared to not despair when things go badly and to not be elated when things go well.

When reinventing oneself, journalists come in handy.

A dinner, sandwiched between Luc Ferry[*] and Alain Minc.[†] Unfortunately, I contend that Nicolas is not fat. Poor thing, says one, you're entangled in totalitarian thinking, the requisite objectivity in your book may well be lacking. You must choose, says the other, either be ambitious or be in love.

. . .

[*] Professor of philosophy and former Minister of Education in the cabinet of Prime Minister Jean-Pierre Raffarin.
[†] Advisory board member of *Le Monde*.

He enters the dressing room, right before the big show on TF1.* Exasperated with the aggregated PR consultants in tow. I will not be followed by assholes I don't associate with, ever. How does that look? A guy arrives with an army of fucking publicists! Leave me alone.

He is upset, but he has to contain himself. He has two hours, live, ahead of him. Edgy, but controlled. Not important. Not true.

True ones, I have never seen. Rages, tantrums left and right, I have been told, furious outbursts, privileges of proximity still inaccessible to me.

They are talking about *turns*. They say, It's my turn, it's not my turn. It's whoever's turn. The one who is elected, he is the one the French think, it's his turn, Jacques told me. A word from day-to-day life that presupposes order, position, legitimate expectation. All things linked to time. Clocks, age. But in the space where swords cross, the turn is an invisible fate.

The church at Saint-Étienne-du-Mont, after communion, politicians emerge, one by one.

Charlotte, wife of Laurent Solly, is dead at thirty-

* French television channel.

five. Her photograph propped on the coffin, a radiant face, which is no more.

The politicians file stiffly past me, as I stand in the back, their faces displaying the same devastation, an expression so stricken that it does not tolerate more than a minuscule grimace in response to my smile, stock sign of recognition, without gaiety but suddenly a shameful defilement, a lack of compassion, of poise.

He throws a rose on the coffin, just lowered. He vanishes. He takes refuge in the backseat of his car, alone. Pierre and Élodie are drifting around. Not knowing what to do. Finally, Pierre approaches and dares to lightly touch the tinted window, barely a furtive tap to say, We're leaving you alone, but we're here.

Tragedy irrupts, into a world devoid of elemental sentiments, into the center of a movement that will not be impeded, tragedy is striking against Laurent Solly, whose arresting beauty is, in itself, something out of a novel.

Laurent, on the phone: "Me, the consummate workaholic, I find myself stalling on the essentials. Now I need to know which way to turn on the slippery slope. Where I'll be forbidden happiness? . . ."

I am stunned by this word uttered on a day of mourning. This word has no gravity on any other day. These men do not want happiness, they want to be given a chance in battle.

I ask Samuel, who attended Saint-Cyr and set his sights on a military career, how he foresees his future. "I don't know. Well, there is the corporate world, or civil service with the Prefecture. Or politics."

"What does that mean?"

"Good question . . ."

Cioran,* in his notebooks, *Whenever I am working for several hours and caught by what I am doing, I don't think at all about "life" or "the meaning" of anything.*

Tour of the Alstom factory of Le Creusot. Inspecting the long corrugated-iron hangars, garish greens and yellows, the big workshops where the bogies are built, splendid shapes and obscure words, reamers, milling gantries, calibrating benches . . . "The chassis that

* Emil Cioran, Romanian philosopher and essayist who moved to France in 1937, friend and contemporary of Eugène Ionesco, Paul Celan, and Samuel Beckett.

young man was working on is the chassis of the future Singapore high-speed train. Makes you feel good, doesn't it?" He has climbed on his little crate, a crate so small that he cannot be seen at all. Luckily, he has a microphone. To Henri de Castries* and Nicolas Baverez† who, during a campaign meeting, earlier in the week, press him to speak to the French service sector, he answers feebly, Yes, yes, of course . . . I'm not the Communist Party candidate if that's what you're trying to say . . .

You have appropriated Jaurès now.
    Yes.

He goes down the rue de Moncennis, entering the butcher shop, the grocery, the bakery, the Café des Sports, the antiques shop, surrounded by a feral pack of journalists, cameras, people in general, so that he misses the window, the smashing window where five women, crammed to catch a glimpse of him, beatific smiles, the middle one very old presumably on her knees, only her dazzled face visible, all in rapture from

---

* President of the French insurance company AXA since May 2000.
† French journalist, economist, lawyer, and author of *La France qui tombe*.

the event, happy to be crammed, crushed against the thin balustrade, happy for the day and for the madness that reigns on the sidewalk.

Farther down, in the clubroom of the retirement home, a little lounge on the ground floor, he says: ". . . Because white hair is a good thing in a neighborhood, in a village." The ladies (there are almost no men) are standing to welcome him, between the card tables and Scrabble games. Each one pin-curled, clipped, and overpermed, the little helmet of golden, chestnut, violet, or red. Not one white head.

On the wall, a bucolic tapestry of a rare violence.

I think of Andrea Peralta, who sacrificed her beautiful years for the love of an anti-Franco colonel. She, too, ended her life among the tables and the games.

There is this photograph of her, taken in the mountains, that my daughter Alta framed, she must be eighty-five years old and has the helmet hair I just described. Knee-high to a grasshopper, a little hunchbacked, she prepares for a hike in an outfit like no other. A turquoise low-neck sweater, out of which pops the scalloped collar of a white shirt, above skintight beige long johns, a dark cardigan tied around her waist, the sleeves dangling as if she were a child. She is posing, her arm resting on a wooden fence, a kind of backpack, game pouch, is hitched on the other shoulder.

Seeing her again in the photograph, I know exactly how she is going to take off on the path, hands free, at an unreasonable speed, ready to fight with the earth, the roots, the wild strawberries, the days left to live, ready to fight.

Advice, consulting, amphetamines for the instinct.

He listens to this, to that, looking at his perpetually crackling fire, foot swinging, he listens through a screen, filtering all but a few elements, he is at the same time with them and within himself, he only retains what hones his conflicting sensibility.

He says, I am willing to mouth off about euthanasia.

Now, you're sure!?

There are limits to suffering, sometimes you have to take a stand. Life doesn't belong to the guy next to the bed. It belongs to the one lying in it suffering.

Such preoccupation, since when? In a race where inventiveness is its own reward, a commercial argument might merge with the most profound idea.

. . .

"Repentance for the colonies"! We should be paying this Jack Lang guy. A gentleman and a scholar!

My notebooks padded with these droll assassinations, laid waste with the turn of a page.

They are sitting around, in a lounge of Hotel Adlon, at a round table.

Before persuading Angela Merkel that a simplified treaty will break the European logjam, Alain Juppé and Nicolas Sarkozy are paving the way with Minister of the Interior Wolfang Schäuble.

. . . I am ready to take a political risk in France, not to have Germany slam the door in my face.

And you intend to say it like that to Angela?

Well, yeah . . . Unless you say I shouldn't. In that case, Alain and I, we're going to go visit the zoo and eat some *apfelstrudel* . . . But I'm going to tell you, Wolfgang, friendship is also a step forward . . .

Absurd stopover at the Holocaust Memorial. Asphyxiated by cameras, microphones, the vulgar pack clambering up on the monuments, they derail, at the edge of the field of steles, without venturing a step into the strange corridors, without knowing where they stand.

. . .

Not a microphone offered, not a question for Alain Juppé. They exit, shoulder to shoulder, onto the windy expanse outside the Chancellery, having left Angela Merkel (black pumps, black pantsuit, and undulating gait I could not have foreseen) on her silent tier. Not a question for Alain Juppé, not a camera lens trained on him. A former Prime Minister, former heir apparent to the President, he is mute and dignified in his brown parka, listening, ignored by everyone, to the repartee of the prosperous young Nicolas.

The conversation drifts to theater and the actors' life:

JUPPÉ: One can be happy playing small parts.

SARKOZY: Write that down, write that down, Yasmina, on February 12, 2007, on the way back from Berlin, Alain Juppé says: One can be happy playing small parts!

JUPPÉ: I didn't say *I* can.

SARKOZY: It's even more serious to have said *one,* it's an attempt to dissemble.

Juppé smiles.

SARKOZY: I've known Alain for thirty-two years . . .

JUPPÉ: Thirty-one.

SARKOZY: He always needs to be right. I don't mind.

JUPPÉ: I am right.

SARKOZY: You see?

Simone Weil, in *Gravity and Grace: Attachment is nothing more than a deficiency in one's sense of reality.*

Could it not be said of the desire for power or glory? I have always seen this desire as the implicit form of that deficiency.

I question G. about his future. As he answers, he slips this in: ". . . otherwise, I'll do something else." This famous something else, so often heard, this opening through which no one ever goes. Words without contours, to mask the extraordinary prison of political destiny.

While I am in the mountains, Nicolas is on the island of La Réunion: "Because my life and the story of my life start from the very bottom and go right to the top. There's only one last step for me . . ."

Right to the top? Is there, in a human life, a place named *the top*? How disenchanting if there were.

Sils Maria.

People walking in nature. It is snowing, small

flakes. A donkey in a paddock. Infinite sadness at having to leave. Leave the pine trees, the larches, the long frozen lakes. I have walked a few feet into the forest with Nathan. Head bare. Snow in his black hair. On the road down, the houses of Engadine, the boulders, the beautiful walks I took. In the distance.

Joys stolen from time. Like all joys.

Resume course, tainted yet vital.

A conversation with the Minister of the Interior in Madrid, whose sole purpose is to reinforce "the friendship." Surrounding the two ministers, around a dark oak table, French ambassador, Michel Gaudin, a security attaché, and a few other Spanish personalities. Mutely looking at unemployed white sheets of paper. The two ministers congratulating themselves, evoking ETA and Islamic terrorism, mutual praise, flattery, conventional words in humorous mode. What's the point? Or is it I who understands nothing? Who fails to appreciate these purely formal moments, and their import? The invisible and imperious code of diplomacy or, in all matters, the necessary nothingness?

.   .   .

He comes to see us in the back of the plane. Pale, tired face. The visit to Madrid has been partly spoiled by an article, defamatory and petty to boot, in the *Canard Enchaîné*. (Not the first time, I notice, he is more affected by his honesty being questioned than by the possible electoral damage.) We speak about the Mediterranean, cradle of us all, a topic dear to him and Guaino, lately. I say, You find Seville more agreeable than Oslo. Berlin! he corrects, you can stop at Berlin! I'm terrified in Berlin! And in Frankfurt too!

He praises Zapatero and Alfredo Rubalcaba, his Spanish counterpart. He also speaks warmly of Blair and Prodi. I say, It's funny that you're pals with these guys from the left. He bursts out, Because they're not from the left! Only French people think you can *live* on the left!

After the international summit, in his dressing room at the Hotel Méridien, the politicians press in, smothering him. Rachida Dati whispers in my ear: "Look, look, how they stick to him. We'd kill our own mothers to sit next to him or be with him in the photo singing "La Marseillaise." I've stopped going up on the stage, I'm afraid I'll get lynched."

.   .   .

I saw again, in New York, *A Spanish Play,* beautifully staged by John Turturro. Eerie impression that this script condenses all that ever interested me in writing. The characters, whatever their age—none of them is young—strive to *stay in the becoming.* To stay in the becoming, obsession of all those to whom I have given a name, a voice. Where does it come from, this heartrending tendency to sense, at the slightest hindrance, that one is an outcast?

In the same play, I rediscover this sentence written four years ago. *The characters are who we are, only better than us.*

He is supposed to have said, I read in the press, coming back from New York: "A presidential campaign, it's tough . . . Because you have to go search deep in yourself for the serenity, the calm, the peace, to keep you from getting carried away. It is a way of forgetting oneself."

He got lost in the words. He probably had in mind to speak of so-called sacrifices and self-restraint.

Forgetting oneself is not what they are living. They are forgetting others; they are, inevitably, self-obsessed.

. . .

At the Henri-Mondor Hospital, in Créteil. A room in Neurosurgery. He is seated beside Xavier Bertrand,* facing some forty members of the hospital staff. A nurse, who more or less initiated this meeting, opens. She brings up, in a trembling, almost inaudible voice, her two little daughters, "apples of my eye" (what are they doing here?), how rough life is, the conditions of . . . the difficulty . . . then she starts crying for no palpable reason. He is embarrassed; he says, I'm not in the habit of making women cry. Behind this quip lies some truth. He is the source of these shameless tears. He, whose prominence and vested power precipitate that inconvenient catharsis.

Another nurse:

. . . There's this dehumanization. There's all this talk about profitability, treatment evaluation, bed turnover. But nobody talks about patient care.

He slips off his jacket.

He writes down some notes . . . He writes just as I do the cold music of consequence . . . *efficient care,*

---

* French politician, current Minister of Labor, Social Affairs, and Solidarity. He was Minister of Health for almost two years in Dominique de Villepin's government under President Jacques Chirac. He announced his support of Sarkozy in September 2006 and quit the government in March 2007 to devote himself fully to the Sarkozy campaign.

perennialization of health care competence, linking costs to activity . . . He takes notes like a studious boy. He takes notes all the more, because he is not listening. Questions keep coming, he will not respond to a single one, precisely. He is agitated, arms constantly moving. His speech is generic, founded on fleeting certitudes, oblivious to the extent he disappoints.

Speaking on pain management, he says, When my mum delivered . . . Later, he says again, When my mum bought her apartment . . . My mum? From what exhaustion could spring such a curious formulation? Attempting to appear human or absurdly leveling with a crybaby.

I have the feeling that he is lost.

Pierre, nothing new? Everything all right, Laurent? Nothing special, Franck? Questions shooting out of nowhere, innocuous demands, which impress me, in the long run, as nothing more than existential supplications. That some grace befall, something *else* . . .

Upon the death of sociologist Jean Baudrillard, I find in the press, in the form of an epigraph, *His desire not to miss anything in life*. An inclination that can lead to the exact opposite . . .

.   .   .

At the Salon de l'Agriculture, where it is absolutely impossible to see him and where the animals, out of their context, have no presence at all, I only retain what the banners read. Among the Red Piebalds of the Plains (they are cows), Revolution is right next to Tisane, and Simone comes from Austria . . .

How to get down in writing the strolling fortress, the dancing canopy of black booms that shadow his smallest step? Since the outset, I have yet to succeed.

"Ladies, set the bar high!" he says to the gentle readers who came to the breakfast of *Femme Actuelle*. Invigorated by his opening line, he has already moved on. Hand on the cell phone, chewing on the tail of a croissant, he listens to the first question with attentiveness all the more solicitous for its absence. The measured tone of the answer lasts all of three minutes. He is galvanized and, bam, bangs on the table, backtracks to the thirty-five-hour workweek "calamity," menaces, wags his finger, and then he reiterates.

In front of "The Presidents of the French Abroad," as I hear him pronouncing yesterday's words exactly, the day before yesterday and an hour ago to the lady readers, with subtle variations and a conviction ever more emphatic, it dawns on me that he is addressing himself.

The places, people, circumstances, don't matter; he is weaving his own material, lapels and cuffs, darted seams, his iron warp and weft. Shining armor of an actor.

Not long ago, Moïra said to me:

Alexander and Genghis Khan, they lived real lives. They gobbled entire territories, they commanded armies, they shed blood. They were retreating for real, they were victorious for real. They were really dying. You were defeated, you were impaled. Politicians today, how do they live?

Monday, March 12. Somber day.

He takes his seat in the little plane. Asks for the ratings of the radio and TV shows he just did. He falls silent, tilting his head back toward the window. In such a way that we too fall silent.

This morning, the polls announce for the first time Bayrou on par with Royal, right behind him. The mood has, perhaps, nothing to do with that. After a while:

Franck? Is there any candy?

He is handed a box of Rimbambelle that he cannot manage to open. Silent and violent struggle against the plastic packaging.

Laurent comes to his rescue.

He eats a piece of the candy and offers me the box without a word.

Errant tour of the immense Airbus site in Méaulte. In the deserted space, uncannily pristine, with neither journalist nor photographer, he allows himself to be guided along the cockpits and sections; he is surly, he stops to look at a worker adjusting a bolt on the door of an A320.

Roundtable with the unions.

". . . if the discussion is about trying to do a *joint venture* so that the Airbus employees will stay Airbusian . . ."

He pronounces it, deliciously, *John Ventura*.

On the plane back. Still somber.

I dare:

Does it still seem a long way off for you?

I don't think about it.

So you live day by day?

Yes. I just think of what I have to get done that day. That's enough.

Silence. He looks at his hands. Then, he adds:

Why even think?

It's a valid question. It could be applied to a lot of things.

Yes. To a lot of things.

Vesoul.

When he enters the tiny room, there is a very small girl holding a violin; in front of a dozen or so cameras and microphones, he says, You, poor little thing! He could not be more sincere. In this *poor little thing,* there is an It's not me forcing you to do this, I too am trapped in this music school visit, it's killing me and it seems like it's never going to end.

At the end of the corridor, the last door opens. He has already suffered Mozart, Presley, Gershwin, Bartók . . . The room is measurably bigger than the others. Aligned, fifteen young musicians (percussion and wind instruments) await the signal of the conductor, a slender woman with short hair, in a blouse. As soon as she raises her arm, an unforeseen liveliness possesses her body. She is possessed by the jazz she has set in motion. She shakes her hips, inebriated by rhythm; she sings above the cymbals' crash, and her flailing arms conduct madly beyond the reeds of the orchestra.

He has positioned himself off to the side. Primed

for a last act of patience. I observe him. He has snapped out of his stupor. He cannot take his eyes off of her, he is bobbing his head, he is smiling like a kid filled with wonder. His best face, in my book.

Facing the UMP parliamentarians, at campaign headquarters:

We have Royal, who's paying a high price for not being head of the Socialist Party. All the same, she's solid. She's a fighter. We have Bayrou, who's running as "Le Pen lite." We have a France that craves amusement like never before. And we have a system that wants to write the history of our demise.

Later.

The same ones who advised me to hire a coach in order to counter the Socialist Madonna, who told me, You see that smile, now look at you, you see the way she laid her hand on that cripple, you really don't get it, you poor schmuck, today those same ones are telling me, Did you see that tractor? Tenure and a tractor, you really don't get it, you poor schmuck. The same ones.*

* The challenger, Bayrou, liked to pose with his farming equipment.

. . .

In Sisteron, he dedicates a plaque "Public Service—Information Bureau." A red circle, stuck on a blue circle, riveted to the wall, where these words are written. He stands, absurdly upright, under this hideous, pathetic, sign, as a crowd crushed behind security barriers sings "La Marseillaise."

Everywhere we go, people are parked behind barriers. It ends up feeling normal. Faces in ecstasy. As he arrives, they stretch out their arms, take pictures.

One day, he encapsulates it all:

Say hello to him! No, no! . . . The child wails, he turns away . . . He likes you! No!! Yes, he does, say hello to him, he's going to be the President . . . I do more kisses for more cameras than Mickey does at Disneyland.

In Upaix, in the shed, the frightened little goats flee upon his arrival on the other side of the wooden stalls.

Laurent hands him a sheet of paper the size of my writing notebook. Scribbled in ballpoint pen, the results of a poll just in, halfway through a controversy on national identity, right before the helicopter takes off.

1st round NS 31 (+4)
SR 24 (−1.5)
FB 22 (−1)
Le Pen 12 (=)

2nd round NS 54 (+2)
SR 46 (−2)

He looks at the page that he keeps holding in his left hand. He says nothing and his face betrays nothing. He looks, through the window, at the shadows of the blades. He puts his hand to his forehead and closes his eyes. In a shirt, legs crossed, jacket on his lap, he falls asleep with the good figures in his fingers. We ascend. Below, the arid heights of the southern Alps and further the snowcapped peaks. I envy this ability to . . . avoid.

Laurent signals Élodie, who is in the back. She crouches next to me and photographs him. When he wakes, he smiles at her, his eyes fixated on the lens, with real sweetness. You're photographing me while I'm asleep, that's pretty intimate. After a while, I say, Élodie and I took the same photo. I just wrote mine. I know what you wrote. You wrote, He was handed a poll, he must be happy, he falls asleep with the paper in his hand . . . I admit that is what I wrote. He points at Pierre and Laurent, They must be happy. If I were in their shoes, I would be happy. I've been happy. I was like them. Victory is sweeter next to the victor.

How much superstition (and how much posing) in these confessional mannerisms?

Half an hour later, he is on the plane, flanked by the same two and Franck. From my seat, I look at him. I hear them laugh about, probably, some stupid little thing. He doesn't laugh. He yawns, half listening, or maybe not. He is quiet, legs stretched out under the table. Like a man comforted by his cats playing around him.

As he is being made up, in the dressing room at the Zénith, right before his speech to the teenage audience (he mentioned to me the day before that the theme was *love* . . .); he calls me over: "How do you pronounce Rilke? It's the kind of thing you must know."

"Just the way you did."

"They say, it's . . . Rilkey."

"You're not German."

"Rilke or Rilkey? I could split it halfway . . ."

"Don't tell me (I also address Henri Guaino, who is

standing by) you're going to quote the *Letters to a Young Poet*?"

"I am . . ."

Visible consternation on my face.

"You don't like it?"

"I have a funny feeling about this speech . . . Love and the *Letters to a Young Poet* . . ."

"Great, she's cheering me on! She's putting me in the right mood, five minutes before I speak to ten thousand people!"

He will say neither Rilke nor Rilkey, but "a German poet." As for the speech, it will confirm my worst presentiments. What kind of emollient potion did Nicolas Sarkozy and Henri Guaino swallow in order to write the word "love" fifty-three times in a paltry thirty pages? In order to write *Youth is the promise of beginnings, of rising suns on still sleeping worlds*? What state of immense fatigue led them to *this incredible need for love that makes the world go round*? Not to mention the little bells and whistles like *You are lucky to be young, because youth is freedom,* or *To be incapable of sharing love is condemning oneself to always be alone.* What happened to these two men, luckily inspired by each other until now, for them to concoct, scorning all restraint and lucidity, this cooing homily?

. . .

Other excerpt, *You are lucky to be young . . . because the future belongs to you.* Is that true? Aside from the tautology, is there still a religion of the future? The characters in Chekhov envied those who were going to live after them.

He undresses. Takes off his jacket, his tie, his shirt. Bare chest in the Airbus that gains altitude on its way to the Antilles, he pulls on a white Ralph Lauren polo shirt, and flips the collar up as if it were a trench coat, leaving it unbuttoned and open at the neck. Ready for a midwinter tennis game (he has also changed trousers), he heads to the back. He spends an hour with the journalists. I glimpse them, huddled, whispering, in a corner of the aircraft; they remind me of the group of Lubavitchers praying next to the toilets on one of my trips to New York.

When he comes back, smiling, in his half-jogging, half-pajama outfit, emblazoned in enormous letters, POLO SPORT (he has made an appearance for the passengers, improvising a little meeting, I am told), he tosses, across the center row: "Passenger poll, 100 percent!

Bravo.

You know what your problem is?

Do I have one?

It's that I observe you a lot more than you think.

No problem. As long as you don't write.

She's not afraid of us, he says, speaking of the stewardess, who smiles as she passes. It's almost humiliating she's not afraid of us. Everybody knows politicians are sex fiends."

To Michel Barnier, who sees me scribbling and shoots him a look: "You better let her be, or you're courting disaster. That's what I think."

Traffic jam between the airport and Pointe-à-Pitre. This is the first journey on the campaign trail plotted at a pace bearing a resemblance to normal life . . . and it feels to me that it's moving in slow motion.

The door to the RFO* studio has shut. A strange silence sets in before going on air. No one says a word. We are only five in the narrow room. Nicolas, a presenter, two cameramen, and I. Élodie has come in for two seconds to take a photo. I am stupefied when, in

---

* The Réseau France Outre-mer is a network of radio and television stations operating in France's overseas departments and territories around the world.

the silence, the presenter performs some facial exercises. His eyes bulge wildly; he executes a few jaw movements, while keeping his pupils fixated as if in shock. I have never seen eyes open so wide. I turn to Élodie. Has she noticed? . . . "He's blind," she whispers discreetly and gravely. Oh, that's why, I say to myself, of course! The interview starts. Élodie is gone. This journalist is remarkable. He senses, in the inflections of the candidate, the hesitations, the openings, anticipates ends of sentences, saves brilliantly, deftly interrupts. His acuity and subtlety are superior to those of the average journalist. I admire the way this guy from Guadeloupe has overcome his handicap; in passing I notice Nicolas tactfully never attempts to impose his message. When I come out of the room, Élodie says to me: "So you read my text message?" I just receive it now as I had set my cell on silent. "He can see."

Night. Meeting in Pointe-à-Pitre.

The "dressing room." Equatorial heat. White tiled floor, neon lights, paint peeling. On a varnished wood plank, wires and cables sprout from a flat-screen TV, wrestle under trestles, shoot up the walls, haphazardly hooked on hinges, to an impossibly high socket.

On-screen, the senator, Lucette Michaux-Chevry, shouts herself hoarse through a microphone already cranked to maximum. She does the warm-up with a variation of "Together, everything becomes possible," screaming the word "possible," as it occurs for the fourth time, with unprecedented violence.

Nicolas is on his feet, speech in hand.

We are sitting right behind him, Élodie, his makeup girl, Marina, and I.

LUCETTE: Nicolas Sarkossssi, a man with a great heart!

NICOLAS: Girls! Did you hear that?

LUCETTE: I am speaking of the man! THE MAN!!!

NICOLAS: Good thing she's taking it easy tonight.

LUCETTE: He stood up against gay marriage!!

NICOLAS: Uh-oh, I didn't see that one coming! What does that have to do with anything?? . . .

Alone, among tall palm trees, just before the trip to Martinique, white shirt, jacket thrown over his shoulder, dark glasses, he is on the phone, chuckling. He looks a little bit naughty, babyish, his neck hunched, and from time to time his right foot paws the ground like a dog. He laughs, wheeling around, a little wobble. Who is that?

Outside the Labourg Furniture Factory, he asks, standing by large slats crisscrossed, a reddish wood, cheap looking:

"What kind of wood is that?

Mahogany.

It's beautiful!"

And by way of congratulation, his hand lands on the carpenter's back with a slap.

From Schoelcher to Trois-Îlets, by boat, night falls fast, the sky a gentian blue hue and the moon in the shape of a ship.

In an interview with Michel Onfray* (who is perfectly capable of saying . . . the *Nietzschean that I aspire to be . . .* and further down . . . *the libertarian that I am*), he puts forth, in reference to pedophilia and suicide, *environment is not everything, the role of the innate is immense.* A neoconservative trope instantly exploited by his detractors. Elsewhere, geneticist Axel Kahn replies: "I find it worrisome that a candidate for the executive office exonerates himself, in advance, from the responsibility for tragedy. As if there were a gene for tragic destiny. There is no gene of tragic destiny."

A beautiful sentence that could be more con-

* French quasi-philosopher who conducted a famous interview with his ideological enemy Sarkozy for *Philosophie Magazine.*

cise. There is no gene of destiny. Neither tragic, nor fortunate.

But it is no less a tyranny to reduce destiny to environment.

He enters the Train Bleu, at Gare de Lyon. It is noon. He has just resigned as Minister of the Interior. At the door of the lounge: "Got anything worse than this . . ."

He has not finished his phrase when he turns around.

"I'm told that I should be mingling with the people and you're putting me in that room back there? What's that about? Who thought of it? Or am I the only person thinking here?" On the platform of the high-speed train headed for Avignon, a group starts screaming as he passes by: "Sarko! President!"

In the compartment, he sits down, the only one in the quartet to do so. He hisses the following, in a frosty voice, the face falsely amicable for the dozens of faces pressed against the windows.

"Who brought in the fucking pollsters with the posters? . . . You guys don't know shit. Can I have a moment of peace? . . . Who did this? . . . Jesus Christ . . . This is pathetic . . . I'd be better off alone."

He is alone. Facing the folding table and the empty

seat across. He need not turn his back to avoid everyone; he looks at nothing, neither the unavailing landscape that goes by, nor the unavailing men. No counselor comes close until summoned by defrocked name, and no sooner than he has spoken, each one bows out.

Through the interstice of the seats, obliquely, I can see his back. I see him turning on his cell phone, turning it off, never going any further than the home page, not texting, not reading, not calling, Louis's face appearing and disappearing dozens of times.

The memo addressed to him regarding this appearance in the Vaucluse begins:

"You are making your first campaign appearance in the Vaucluse, followed by the Bouches-du-Rhône. The target of this two-day trip is to cut away from the ministerial image and project the peaceful image of a candidate intent on listening to the French people."

Where is he at? asks a man in the street of Saint-Didier, first stop of the peaceful tour of the candidate.

Must be over there. Where it's moving most.

See him? asks a third one.

He's caught in a trap. He's so small, how y' expect me to see'm?

I don't see nothing, complains a woman.

You can't see him, he went in, he went inside the Séduction Coiffure.

They finally discern him, from afar, on the stairs of the Town Hall, doing his little speech ". . . in my day, people used to say, 'Idle hands are the Devil's workshop . . .'" (which day is he talking about?). It is 5:30 p.m., time for applause and to sing "La Marseillaise" on the village square.

He ducks into his car. Citizens, shopkeepers, bystanders stare at the shadow that gathered them as it goes away.

Night. Hamlet of Les Baux.

He just had dinner with Jean-Louis Borloo,* whose support has yet to be confirmed, and Jean-Michel, in a private room.

(Just like Molière's famous catchphrase "And Tartuffe?," in my last winter notebooks, "And Borloo?" persists and punctuates the days, the meetings. "And Borloo?" met only by sighs, shrugs, and, once, the preposterous "I'm biding my time," for answers . . .)

We join them in the lounge, Laurent, Frédéric, David, Franck, Élodie, and I.

* French politician, then a contender for the presidency, currently the Minister of Ecology and Sustainable Development and Planning.

Jean-Louis Borloo (finally in the flesh) wears a pink V-neck cashmere sweater over a white shirt. Nicolas, a gray cashmere sweater-vest over a blue shirt. (To what shall I attribute this curious artificial Irish casual look?)

They face each other from opposite ends of a three-seat sofa. Nicolas, apart, in keeping with the mood *du jour,* Borloo, with Jean-Michel and Frédéric on his side.

Why do I have to go lunch tomorrow with parliamentarians that I see all the time? . . . I have five teams with nothing better to do than beat the living daylights out of one another . . . I'm knocking myself out campaigning while everybody else is knocking themselves out to get in my way.

Silence.

He pronounces these words to those concerned, profiting from the presence of this distinguished witness, with a deadpan cruelty.

Everything weighs on him. And leaves him indifferent. I can read the weight and the indifference on his weary face. Borloo inclines his head, drinks his rosé. I would like to weigh this inclination.

Everyone is silent. Nicolas sinks into his sofa.

Suddenly, Jean-Louis Borloo takes a sheet out of a file, goes over to Nicolas: "Is that you there?" *That* is the official photograph, with a green hill in the background (the one seen everywhere for the last three months). "Is that you there?" he repeats, still standing, tapping the photograph with his fingers. "That is you!" Nicolas, bewildered, looks to Franck. Most of the people present had expressed, at some point, reservations regarding this picture of a sweet boy, long-headed, mimicking an enigmatic Mona Lisa smile. Starting with Jean-Michel, who told him, in January at Porte de Versailles, That doesn't look like you. Nicolas went ahead. He liked this photograph. And even if he wasn't quite sure, his family liked it. Borloo continues: "That's not you. That's not you! . . . (flicking the sheet with disgust) . . . Could we please have a photograph that might be HIM? HIM?"

Nicolas, drooping and dead-eyed, looks at it . . . And in a dull voice: "Okay . . . so Franck, what are we doing? . . ."

One a.m.

Jean-Michel, whose ease and liveliness contrast sharply, says to him: "Take your time tomorrow in Marseille, fool around, go out . . ." (the advice "fool around" to Nicolas Sarkozy, that night, is exquisitely poetic).

I'm doing Canal +.* I can't stay out late.

Is he thinking, legs stretched out under the table, looking at his feet, all crunched up, in a stupor? How much has he registered from his first day as the peaceful candidate, high-speed train, local roads, and strawberry pickers? Not to mention his dinner date with Borloo, who should have pledged allegiance weeks ago.

Wait a minute, Jean-Louis, why don't you go, instead of me, tomorrow?

Good, very good! bursts out Jean-Michel (stifling a laugh!), while you're eating aioli in Marseille!

Tomorrow, I will announce to the press, Jean-Louis has joined me, continues Nicolas in a modulated voice, vaguely morose, exhibiting that refined genius for ignoring others, and by the way he's going to do Canal + instead of me.

Jean-Louis Borloo turns to me: "So what do *you* think?" A final touch to an incongruous scene. Turning a blind eye to the abyss (am I really supposed to get involved? Of course not), I venture a reply.

Nicolas remains stoic:

Franck, all the journalists are waiting at the gate, go confirm that I'm here with Jean-Louis. And that

* French premium pay television channel.

everybody has his own room, he adds. Jean-Michel is
the only one who laughs.

They are left alone there, looking at each other.
    After a while, Nicolas:
    Happy?
    I'm very relaxed, is Borloo's curious answer.
    He moves over to join Nicolas on his sofa.
    They mutter imperceptibly. And then, spent, they
wallow in proximity, as artificial as it is inescapable.

In Marseille, lunch, after a roundtable with the readers
of La Provence, ends right before dessert. He has done
as told, swapped members of parliament for readers of
La Provence, but he couldn't care less about lunch with
readers of La Provence, just as he couldn't care less
about lunch with members of parliament.

On his little dais, words come to the rescue of his
weariness, as they fall through the microphone onto
the workers, the rows of tools, the machines. One day,
in Mexico, I saw a peasant along a deserted road
plunge alone into the forest, with his machete. I think,
listening to his hoarse voice, chopped, in the factory of
marine engines, of the thousand and one ways that
men have to cut their way through.

. . .

He is consistently in the lead. All the polls, for weeks, show him lapping the others in the first round, as well as the second. He continues to say, I consider myself a challenger. I want to stay in the challenger's shoes.

He says it sincerely.

To be the favorite, what a disenchantment for a lover of adversity.

Talking about his team:

They have no right to complain. I've stuffed them. Not spoiled them, stuffed them. Today I need some space, it's not a question of liking or not liking. You can't let yourself be like . . . in normal life if you want to be President of the Republic.

All my life, people have told me not to be in a hurry . . . always wait! And then, one day, you're old and all you've done is wait, he says, in *Philosophie Magazine,* to Michel Onfray (who is perfectly capable of stating, *I am not familiar with boredom, I find life magnificent, saturated with passion . . .*). He picked this phrase out of *In Arthur Schopenhauer's Toboggan: A man once said to me about a dress I had altered, the dress can wait, can wait for what, I retorted . . .* This Wait for what?, he has repeated it often, in different contexts, he has even inserted it in a speech. In reality, it is the What?, which is without end.

Look at the ocean of your fans, jokes Henri, in Nice, in the dressing room, gesturing toward the TV. I point out to Nicolas that he is wearing his pink shirt, which shows perspiration on camera.

He shrugs, he can't be bothered to change. "Or, at the end, I suggest to him, throw it into the crowd, like Johnny."*

"The poor man's Johnny, is that it? The poor man's Johnny, you know what he's got to say to you?"

"This modesty of yours, it's totally missing in what I have written so far."

"That's your mistake."

Hot little truffle rolls, scallops with truffles, butterflied langoustines, truffle pasta, risotto . . . we are served the most exquisite dishes, one after the other, at extravagant speed. He said he wouldn't stay long, he didn't have time, he had to get back to Paris fast. He says to me, Taste this, taste that, fabulous, marvelous, you know me, who knows everything, this is *the* place

---

* Johnny Hallyday, French singer and actor.

in France, so listen, listen! I take Yasmina Reza to La
Petite Maison, they serve her . . . a truffle sandwich,
and she says to me, Love the tapenade! To his right, the
young blonde, showing shoulder, tells him every
night she dreams about him. He whispers to me, she's
telling me every night I dream about you. Isn't that
stunning? I say, uh, yes . . . Listen, that's really touching (letting his hand wander down the back next to
him . . .). I say, touching might not be the word . . .
What, she's adorable, this girl! Do you see how that's
decked out? Nothing cheap there, and have you had
the white chocolate mousse? . . . I say, Nicolas, behave,
don't forget you want to be President . . . He laughs his
child's laugh, he strokes his head, a bit troubled, leaving is forgotten, the girl is pressed against him, he
drinks his limoncello, he says, This place is magic,
everything is magic. Tonight.

It is never too late. One of the first things G. ever said
to me. I understood it as it's not too late, I didn't pay
attention to never.

He's mistaken. No space in life opens as far as the
eye can see.

My notebook in the last few days. So much repeti-
tion. In my notebook, days fingered like beads, blur-

ring, monotonous frenzy where history is still being written.

There are no places in tragedy. There are no hours either. Just dawn, dusk or night.

"I sat on the fence about coming," he says, taking off his jacket, rue Cuvier, in a room at the Natural History Museum, opening the private meeting with the ecological NGOs. "Many of my friends didn't want me to, they thought it was kind of embarrassing . . . I'm willing to debate, but don't bombard me with petitions and tell me, sign, sign, sign, that isn't good enough. As far as bias goes, I bet I'm less biased than some of you are about me . . ."

Upon which the discussion begins, in a fairly constructive way, on both sides. A little bit later, a participant wanting to show appreciation: "Look, you're not a fascist and we're not a bunch of hippies . . ."

"Look, hippies are one thing . . . But watch your mouth with the F-word! You realize how crazy French politics has gotten, when these are our choices!"

In *L'Express,* a piece on him, I find this expression does him justice. *This annoying authenticity* . . . The terms and their juxtaposition do him justice.

. . .

In the bowels of RTL, right before *Le Grand Jury,* he sits in a bright red armchair under a TV mounted on the wall, muted, tuned on LCI.* While he is complaining about his treatment on the airwaves (just as, it seems, every opponent before him), a close-up of François Bayrou, just above his head, laughs in a Martinique market, Ségolène and her scarf float in an Ardèche landscape, and finally, most surreal, him exiting his car, outside this very studio, displaying an ease that he must have lost in the staircase.

Together. Title of his new book, concocted in the utmost secrecy. Nearly the entire staff makes an appearance at the UMP, at sunset, to bring, under the watchful eyes of gods, a copy of the book to three principals from *Le Monde.*

Veranda. Two chairs. A love seat. Coffee table. *Together* placed in front of each journalist. Nicolas (one has to imagine the velvet voice and the tone deliberately stripped of nuance): . . . Here it is. Nobody has it, nobody knows what's inside.

---

* La Chaîne Info, French premium pay television channel.

PHILIPPE RIDET: Thanks . . . No autograph?

NICOLAS: An autograph? Wouldn't that be hypocritical?

The chosen journalists flip through their books. Pages turn in silence.

NICOLAS: . . . Major work . . . It's in the first person . . . You'll see, it's a great . . . You'll read it tonight . . . You'll be up all night . . .

RIDET: You marked the parts where it's verbatim? . . . (Nicolas smiles, magnanimously) . . . Well, okay . . . Anything else you want to tell us?

NICOLAS: What? It's not that bad . . . (he seizes a copy) . . . I stand behind this book. I think this is great too, the cover.

ONE OF THE OTHER
TWO JOURNALISTS: Very presidential.

NICOLAS: Yeah.

Silence.

Some supplementary exchanges follow, the minor kind, bastardized attempts to give some degree of substance to this meeting.

On his feet, walking in the direction of the elevator and, in extremis, regaining his habitual volubility, he says to Philippe Ridet: "You've been convinced, since 2004, that I chose the wrong strategy, what can I say? You think you know everything and a written apology is in order when you fall on your face!"

Again. Again one of these surreal visits with bonnet and white apron, ridiculous caterpillar of a hundred or so following each other through a pastry factory. All is white, walls, ceiling, fabricated from undulating plastic, not a trace of a cake to be seen, maybe they ride the conveyor belt above. To see Borloo, Douste-Blazy,* and Sarkozy while they endure, poor things, several stops to sample some uncooked dough, journalists and their feral equipment sneak in, infiltrate, under the metal chutes, between the electric armoires of a refrigerated hell.

Seated at a table, finally in a well-heated narrow office, under a company poster and an armoire of baguettes and croissants, he devours a chocolate roll, the spirit having deserted the body, feigning as he listens to a

* Philippe Douste-Blazy, Minister of Health under President Chirac.

woman tell him about her "obstacle course" from a famous candy factory (a name he is compelled to write down), all the way up to the position of Hospice Helper. At one point, he feels he should say something and, choking down a chunk, peeking at his pad, brow furrowed like someone worried sick: "So you're telling me you went from 'Gummy Bears' to 'Life Savers'?"

"Within the framework of the CTP I chose to work in domiciles, I adore old people, but as I go from CDD to CDD, I have to leave the CTP . . ." He has configured his lips in a kind of ingenious listener's smile, somewhere between wow and compassion. He can hold this pose frozen for a few minutes and say, at the end, as he does, with a certain gravity: "Thank you, Martine."

Political meeting.

Shirt, white stripes. Shoes, tasseled.

There's too much of everything and not enough in the pot. This is the French state of mind, in a nutshell.

The leg jiggles, the tassels do a jig.

I'm telling you one thing. Without the National Identity issue, we would be trailing Ségolène. We're in the first round, my friends. We're in the first round. If I am at 30 percent, it means that we're raking in Le Pen voters. If Le Pen's people leave me, we sink like a stone.

Tassels flapping in panic.

Taping the official campaign spots.

He arrives, immediately unbearable. Okay, I have no idea what we're doing here, that bugs the shit out of me, and I want to leave as soon as possible. He disappears into the makeup room. Comes out again. Can we get some of these people out of here? It's a train station in here! He sits on a studio chair. Where do I look? Center camera. Okay, ready? Taping of the first clip. "Fellow countrymen . . ." I don't know who found such a repulsive piece of shit for a chair. It's unnatural. I have no information, nothing, no one tells me anything. What are all these people doing here? Clear them all out, I'm sick of this. (He is clearing me out too, but I take no offense. I will stay out of sight.) He tapes several spots in a row. He speaks without notes, without rehearsal, he barely glances at what has been prepared for him and never needs more than two takes. One can only admire his gift, his competence. But what I like, this morning, oddly, is his mood. Not his talent, but how intractable he is, how reluctant he is about compulsory drills, how he detests the rules. What I like also is the low voice, contained, all the more subdued. Okay, what's left? Solidarity? What kind of fucking theme is that? Solidarity, it doesn't mean anything. Someone suggests that he changes his jacket. No, no, I'm fine, I'll stay like this. These are going to be aired three times a day and you want to be dressed the same? Yeah, yeah, this is a nice jacket. He tapes the spot on solidarity. He should smile a little, mutters Jean-Michel, but then, if you ask him to smile, you're going to send him into an indefinite state of rage. Nicolas goes back behind the curtain. He consents to reshoot the first one, judged too aggressive, just as he consents to change his shirt. Say a nice word to the technicians, slips in Jean-Michel. No, no, no, we'll see about it after, that's not my problem. You know you're cramming into an hour and a half what other people take five hours to do. I don't give a shit about other people. Nevertheless, before leaving, he will go talk to the technicians . . . He explains away his attitude as resolve to concentrate and get energized, same as you, guys, you know, it has to go fast! No apology.

Lyon-Bron. Airport.

A group of demonstrators is, apparently, in front of a pastry shop in La Croix-Rousse, where he is expected.

We laugh at stupid things, waiting in the parking lot, under a perfect sun. Eating macaroons in a fancy place was well worth the trip! says José Frèches.* You go to factories, you have the guys from the trade unions, and nothing happens. You go to a pastry shop and you get a demonstration!

As we speak, I see him in the hall, through the windows, pacing, phone to his ear, seething.

When asked about the fact that he has failed to make himself loved, he answers, brandishing the polls, And where would we be if they loved me! Or he says, I go everywhere, to the towns, the factories, all over the country, there's never a demonstration. Distortion of reality, which he believes partly, because he is so protected.

On the other hand, he is capable of saying, Getting elected is not the same thing as getting loved.

I admire this pirouette of pride that spins the object of suffering into a noble statement.

Coming back from Lyon, Henri asks for my opinion on the speech regarding cultural issues.

* French historical novelist.

You're moralizing. But that's the direction that you've been taking lately.

You don't understand politics!

Some apprentice upholsterers nail armchairs in front of I don't know how many cameras and other devices, in the supernatural white noise of hammers banging. He nods. Just as he nods, mute and running out of white lies, half an hour later, looking at a man restoring an antique brick, with a dreadful scraping noise. How many samples, demos, casting, uncasting, hammers, trowels, scrapers? He's been watching old bricks get polished for thirty years, says Laurent.

This Thursday, April 12, in Tours, he makes, in my eyes, his strongest speech since January 14 . . . *Yes, I am the child of immigrants. Yes, I am the son of a Hungarian and the grandson of a Greek, born in Salonica . . . Yes, I am a Frenchman, of mixed blood, who believes that one is French only to the extent of the love one has for France, of the attachment one has for its universal values . . . France is not a race, is not an ethnicity . . . One is not French because of his roots, because of his ancestors . . . One is French because one wants to belong . . . because one is proud of belonging to France. Because one feels obligations to France, because one feels gratitude, grateful to France.*

When we were children, my father, born to Iranian parents in Moscow, married to a Hungarian, declaimed poems of Victor Hugo and La Fontaine . . . *on an ascending path, sandy, uneasy, and on all sides to the sun exposed* . . . he repeated the words, he pointed out the percussive sound of the language, its musicality, he was obsessed by correct pronunciation, he said a man is judged by his accent, I was not allowed to say yeah in front of him, he said, Look at Paris, children, look at Paris, the most beautiful city in the world, you are lucky to live in the most beautiful city in the world, when we were passing by the Invalides, each time he would say, Look at the loveliness of this dome, you want to take it in your hand, it is like a jewel, a ring, you were born in France, this garden, this land of plenty, I hope that you are proud of it, he would recite names from literature (I have written on this), which he might have read, but the way he would quote them was more important than the knowledge, he would quote the writers, the politicians, Talleyrand, Mazarin, he would quote Jaurès (as well), Blum, Raymond Aron, and Mendès France. He had made French history *his* history. At school, friends would say, I'm from Bretagne, I'm from Alsace, I didn't understand these divisions, I said, if I were asked, I'm Iranian, a passport from nowhere, from a country that didn't exist anymore for anyone, my family was scattered beyond the seas, I had no common language with them, but mine, French, was beautiful and had begotten me.

Enchantment, opening the paper.

"I like to be shaken, stirred, whether it's by Cristo's wrapping, Jeff Koons's Puppies, or Varini's anamorphoses," Nicolas Sarkozy, an interview with *Arts Magazine,* quoted in *Le Figaro*.

O joy! O delight, that innocent dive into cultural correctness, which he ceaselessly assails, in each and every speech! What a gift to us, we who know him, that he, under the wing of some mindless counselor, would permit *that* to be published!

Recess.

A tea at Grandma's.

I ask whom she intends to vote for. It's really bothering me, she says. Bayrou, certainly not. I will certainly not vote for a man who put his wife through six children. He is inconsiderate. Le Pen, well, we know very well the opinions of that old stick-in-the-mud. Ségolène, I could just slap her. For me, I'm going to tell you, she could be at Franck & fils, thirty years ago, telling me, Madame M., I have a pretty little blue dress that is so you. We used to call that a premier, premier sales lady, now we say sales manager, just like maids are now called surface technicians. Marie-George is nice and she is no idiot. I won't vote for her but I like her. She is a woman I could meet at the market and invite over for coffee. Nicolas is too high-strung. Having a son like mine, I know high-strung when I see it. He is four inches too short and that undermines his charisma on the international level. Mitterrand, you couldn't tell he was short because he was placid, whereas Nicolas is a fox terrier running everywhere, barking. The guy whose name ends in *i,* the old one with the southern accent, for me he could be selling Corsican donkey sausage at La Baule-les-Pins, he would be perfect. José Bové,* first of all I will not do anything for him until he shaves off that mustache. The pipe, I would break it in half, crack! A mustache and a pipe, two things I can't stand about that man. In the early days of José Bové, I had a kind of sympathy for the guy, he was a rebel, setting fire to all those places that serve shit. Since then, no. For me, he is a

---

* French farmer and syndicalist, member of the antiglobalization movement, and spokesman for Via Campesina. He was one of the twelve official candidates in the 2007 presidential election.

zero now. And when does he find time to be a farmer? Voynet,[*] she's sweet, but then, well, when she is speaking to me, Voynet, about the ozone layer, I pay attention. But when she speaks to big industry, who cares? They don't give a damn about Dominique Voynet. You know, there's not a lot of them who find favor in my eyes.

But then whom will you vote for?

Well, I am going to vote for little Sarkie, she sighs.

On the flight to Toulouse.

I say, I still love the men I have loved.

He shrugs as if I were saying an unbearable stupidity.

Yes. I assure you. I never stopped loving the men I loved.

Oh please!

I still love them, differently.

It's all in the differently, darling. Don't treat me like a moron. When you start qualifying love, it stops being love.

[*] Dominique Voynet, French senator for the department of Seine-Saint-Denis, member of the Greens, and their candidate for the 2007 presidential election.

Rather sharp exchange with a CGT leader, in an Airbus administration building.

I like you, Daout, but when you land an uppercut, you better expect one in return. That said, I've thought about all this a lot . . .

One of his aids whispers to me, When he says, I've thought about all this a lot, it means that he hasn't at all.

In the corridor of the Claudius-Regaud Cancer Institute, among the crowd of followers, I hear this sentence pronounced by a pleasingly plump woman in a suit, hair dyed red, about fifty: ". . . A neighborhood hospital, with the old people in the city." She says it as if she were speaking of another species, and we always say that kind of thing, the old people, without ever thinking that one day we will be them.

I have pinned on my wall a photograph taken by Élodie during an appearance in the Bay of Somme. It's raining, a woman holds a large black umbrella above him. He is looking at a wing-flapping falcon, talons held by a man's hand. He is staring at the bird and recoiling with a frightened and stupefied expression that I see in his face again in front of the linear accelerator, the ultramodern spinning radiotherapy machine, inside of which lies a leather dummy.

Libération headline, April 12: Interview with Nicolas Sarkozy, "Capturing the National Front Vote: Is It a Bad Thing?," accompanied by a photograph, finger pointing.

The exact sentence, in the article, is: "In whose book is capturing the voters of the National Front a bad thing?"

Is it the same *thing*?

Once again (last time, I promise!), in the interview with Michel Onfray (who is perfectly capable of writing in his blog, as he recounts the meeting, *It is as if I am Seneca sitting in Nero's apartments*), he says, *Me, I had to transgress certain rules to create my persona . . .* He doesn't say, I forged myself, or I built myself, he says, I created my persona.

In the dressing room, in Toulouse.

NICOLAS SARKOZY: Elegant, your suit.
PHILIPPE DOUSTE-BLAZY: Prada.
NICOLAS SARKOZY: Beautiful material,
beautiful cut. (Seeing me).
We're talking threads.

Colombey-Les-Deux-Églises.

Meditation on the tomb of the General.

Entering La Boisserie. (What is he doing when he disappears behind the foliage? A mystery.)

Reappearance. Solitary ascent in the allée, under the branches . . . (the left leg is twisting, he hasn't yet mastered the pensive walk in the shadow of great trees).

Station, in front of the gigantic and hideous cross of Lorraine, with projected shadow.

Solemn inscription in a visitors' book of three neo-historical phrases, in a silence imposed by the presence of a France 2 microphone (the sole apparatus, due to the event's quasi-confidential atmosphere).

Noon. In the land of signs, in a village of Haute-Marne.

Metz.

He is observing the welding of a hot-water tank. Eyes at half-mast. I know very well he is not listening to the explanation. He has not listened to any explanation, and it does not matter, while walking alongside the tubes, the aisles of tubes folded in accordance with mysterious movements, the bottoms of tanks piled on top of each other, the violet steel sheets, looking like mattresses. One could write anything about that absent face, staring at the cylinder pressed on both sides, forever smothered. One could also write about the destiny of things made of metal. A few days ago, he said, referring to a fictionalized history book, Imagination is as true as reality. What Daladier had in mind, no one knows. Nobody knows. He didn't even know himself.

Nine a.m. In Saint-Ouen. He is sitting outside a café, striped shirt, polka-dot tie. He is answering the readers of *Le Parisien*. A last stunt, after dozens of the same kind. I feel he is spent, nervous. He is verbose, flaunts himself, gives an all-too-polished impression, pointlessly shows off, indulges in a kind of cheap pedantry that signals exasperation. A woman asks: "Why do you keep losing your temper every time someone asks something?"

"In France, political life is suffering from a deficit of sincerity, of passion, Brigitte . . ."

"You can be calm and sincere at the same time."

"You have to be ready to grunt when you're disgruntled, Brigitte."

"You are not grunting, you are growling."

He softens his reply, throwing in one or two extra ineffective "Brigitte"s, because Brigitte hates him.

Strange week of media backlash. Random sampling of headlines and excerpts from articles, "Vote Fear," "The Alarming Mr. Sarkozy," "Stale smell of prewar Stalinist propaganda and fascist rhetoric," "So frightening is the character," "Most pitiless politician in Europe," "This is a madman! Who exhibits the kind of madness that has fueled the ambition of many a dictator in our past." Words weakened nonetheless by the accompanying photographs, ranging from shifty to forbidding, to demonic or Hitlerian. As if the blackness of these penned portraits, in spite of the ink's thickness, lacked density and needed to be reinforced by images.

Patrick Devedjian:

We don't want to look death in the eye. We're in the midst of the battle. See, decay can't close in. We don't let it get near. We believe we can outrun decay.

But you think you can outrun anything.

Yes, we do.

Last major meeting, in Marseille.

In the dressing room, two screens side by side. The first one shows images of the hall. The front row, Fillon, Juppé, Borloo . . . almost all of his political allies. He is happy, relaxed, his brother François is there, with his wife and a friend. He is looking at the screen, satisfied by the presence and number of personalities. The second TV is tuned to LCI, which is broadcasting his meeting in Issy-les-Moulineaux, the night before. He doesn't pay attention at all. Suddenly, he exclaims, Look, look what they're showing! Basile's header!!! We see footage of the 1993 Europe football championship, and Basile Boli* heading the ball into the goal. Who appears in the flesh, onstage, to ovations from the crowd. Look at Basile! He's going to speak, he's the one who is going to speak now! He can't contain himself. Look at the room! And David Ginola!!† El Magnifico!! Look, it's him!!! He's never made a speech, Basile, and now he kicks off with eighteen thousand people! He glances at himself on the other screen, And me, what the fuck am I doing? He gestures for that TV to be turned off, he is looking at Basile Boli enraptured, popping a little pill with some sparkling water and asking politely for still water, he combs his hair, he says, You know Ginola, he's an idol for a lot of people. Look, look at the crowd, as far as the eye can see!! He laughs. It's a laugh

---

* Former French soccer player and current television sports presenter.
† Former French international soccer player and a model.

for no particular reason, a laugh of hollow content-
ment, like the one a child could have.

I listen to the speech in the dressing room with
Bernard Fixot. I note down these two boasts, *If I didn't
exist, someone would have to invent me* and *I know nothing
of the avarice of sentiment.*

On the way back, I confirm with Henri that neither
was in the final draft.

The next day I will ask him the same question—I
don't use "boasts," I use "phrases"—he hurries to
answer that they are, of course!, his, he doesn't hear
the little irony bell tinkling and goes on and on, the
predictability nearly numbing, yes, it's true I know
nothing of the avarice of sentiment.

This morning, last day of the official campaign before
the first round, I hear Ségolène Royal on France Inter.
*It was taboo, Blair shouldn't be quoted . . . I would like to
maintain the freedom . . .*

Two traits in common, emancipation and lifting
taboos.

On the phone, late at night, G., from the provinces,
contests the sagacity of certain of Nicolas's statements.
When one wants to be president of the Republic, he
preaches, one does not say this or that. I should speak

in depth about it with him because it is the opposite that looks me in the face. When aiming at that position, it is precisely what is not supposed to be said that one says and nothing is more welcome than scandal.

When he enters, he is on horseback, red checked shirt, jeans, Camargue's black bulls as backdrop, in front of our warbling tractor-pulled cart transporting roughly fifty journalists who are supposed to follow him on his outing. He removes his Ray-Bans. Nicolas, who cannot stand daylight, is quickly blinded and blinks amid the cameras. Among the enigmas that compose his person, this one: why opt for this oblong, opaque porthole design (Joe Pesci, on a street in Palermo), preventing any reasonable presentation of his person in shades?

Back from Saintes-Maries-de-la-Mer, nearly no one aboard. Élodie and I are sitting across from him. I ask him if he is moved or anxious, twenty-four hours before the first-round ballot. "Less than I thought. There's been no drama. I did everything I had to do. I did it all the way."

I realize that it is precisely what moves me. He does everything he has to do. All the way.

He is not waiting for help from above.

. . .

Chirac called me: I am very optimistic. I wouldn't have said that to you four days ago. I am very optimistic. I wouldn't have said that four days ago, he said to me.

He snatches one of Élodie's cameras from the table, the loaded one, with the large cannon, to see "how it feels to see someone through this." He looks at her through the lens, trains it on her. The opposite of what I have observed for months.

He frames and shoots.

It is a surprising image, it is inverted, a wrinkle in time. Élodie is embarrassed, adorable.

I listen to very few people. And they don't tell me to be nice. I don't need people to tell me to smile, to reassure. I wish you knew how much I don't need this. I hate—and that's a weak word—to be told that stuff. They are only repeating something they read in the paper and they can take away your confidence in a week.

Sunday, April 22. 18 rue d'Enghien.

Around 5 p.m. in Laurent's office.

He is on the phone with a pollster: Narrow

between us and her? What have you got? . . . (He hangs up.) This crook will not give numbers! These assholes, it bugs the shit out of us to have to deal with them all year long, *you are too temporal, you should be more spiritual,* spiritual, these assholes! And now they won't give a fucking number.

The whole parliament is calling Lefebvre, he's saturated with phony phone calls!

So?

It's like waiting for a tsunami in a tunnel. So far we are still alive.

Samuel says to me, You win either way. No matter what. And if we don't make it to the second round, you're the real winner. You'll have yourself a real tragedy.

I am keenly aware of the absurdity of the word "winner."

This work, bitter and nontriumphant, cannot be otherwise.

And none other more than this one.

Around 5:30, I show myself in the door frame of the little meeting room at the very moment he too arrives.

He is tense and at once requests the door shut. I dare, May I stay? I am expecting a No Yasmina, please! But instead he says, Come in! I am a wallflower with a notebook. Around the table, the political team (twenty or so, minus Alain Juppé) is silent. He says, For now nothing is certain, Ipsos just compiled the exit poll . . . shut the door! People are either in or they're out! That's it! This is not a train station! . . . (Xavier Bertrand and Philippe Douste-Blazy will be locked out a for a while) . . . Giacometti* tells me, the first rank has been written in the sand. Okay. Anything can happen. (A telephone rings) . . . Phones off, for fuck's sake . . . Giacometti says: We know the first two, it's her and me. If Le Pen is low, our strategy is good. If we are above 25, it's very good, above 27 it's great, above 28 is golden . . . (his cell phone vibrates) . . . Voter turnout 80 percent! When I think of all the dipsticks who called our campaign worthless! Now you can say I had the face to face the issues.

At 5:50, he takes a call on his cell phone and, muttering, leaves the room. He comes back a few minutes later, okay, Giacometti, who is no joke, will have more in ten minutes, but it looks like we are around 30 percent. It is historical. He suddenly brightens: If

* Pierre Giacometti, head of Ipsos, the polling organization.

we're at 30 percent in a country where 85 percent have voted, it's a tidal wave! . . . He smiles. He turns this way, that way, it's contained but genuine happiness. Maybe the moment of relief is the happiest moment. In the meantime, do you want me to read you my announcement?

I reread the notes taken during this hour. There is only him, his voice, his words. He is alone. That's him being called, receiving figures, informing the others, him who analyzes, instructs, entertains. His aides are absent, except for Claude Guéant, condemned to record continuously mysterious notes. No filter between him and the thing. The hour is his, the day is his.

He rehearses his imminent announcement, seated at the oval table, in front of the little political committee. He intones, the energy, the will to persuade. They applaud. He says, Result of a night with Henri. Me and Guaino are going to end up having a baby. I adore him. But spending the night with him kills me. I had rather something else . . . Okay, but I owe him a lot. When we are facing each other, just the two of us, sometimes, we have tears in our eyes.

At 6:45, he comes back (he has again gone out to answer a call), Kids, kids (from now on he will not stop saying kids), now it is not polls but estimates on the ballot. Us 31, Sego 25–26, Bayrou 17, Le Pen 11. Ovations for Le Pen 11. He leans toward Simone Veil, kisses her, My little talisman, she's not the easiest but . . . It should be Simone who speaks to them, the Le Pen supporters, if it's me who says, I thank you for having left the ogre, it loses something! . . . Kids, let's stay focused, we're still in the first round until the announcement. For me, it's the culmination of five years, I would even say twelve years of work . . . CSA* 31! The nice people at CSA, five more points in twenty-four hours! I'm out of here, I'm going to see the family!

He exits the room.

Beautiful weather, Monday, April 23.

Nicolas has not arrived. Outside, the dead-end in front of the Coeur de Femmes association, the founder, a woman who welcomes women in precarious states, introduces Simone Veil to some of them.

So, are you cozy with Mr. Sarkozy?

Later.

Madame, if we welcome the whole Congo, there

---

* Another major polling organization.

won't be a Congo left. I want those who are welcome to be truly welcomed. If you welcome all of Africa, who will live there?

Some French people, answers the woman.

Enrico, you have your guitar?

On a plane, you can't hear anything.

You'll see what I'm going to say about Algeria! I would have liked to be in Algeria. Born in North Africa, you were dreaming of France, born in Paris, you didn't dream of anything!

Dijon. Onstage, Enrico Macias* sings *Sarko, you took me in your arms*. In the dressing room, looking at him on-screen, he starts clapping his hands, abandoning the speech he just received to better listen. Then, all of a sudden he gets up and asks me to dance.

We dance, delighted. Élodie snaps the picture.

Before his own appearance, Eric Besson, ex–national secretary for economic issues at the Socialist Party, is onstage. A man who began the campaign on Ségolène Royal's team, and finishes it supporting Nicolas Sarkozy. I look at him, gesturing on-screen, fascinated

* Algerian-born French singer.

by the singular transgression, the spectacle we're watching . . . *The only hope of beating him was to demonize him, to caricature him, so he would inspire fear . . .*

I say, This is good. To which Nicolas responds as he is leaving the dressing room, Hey you, you are not here to admire other people!

LAURENT: What could we do for May 4? Last day of the official campaign? What would it be, that ultimate image, any ideas, Yasmina?

Y.: A drink at the Palais-Royal with one great writer.

PIERRE: Uh-oh, the return of the recorder!

LAURENT: We had "Lisa Simpson playing the sax" and now we have "Yasmina playing politics."

They are standing in a semicircle in front of him, corolla of ties and serious faces (a few women). Leaning on the railing of the third floor of rue d'Enghien. I observe him from above galvanizing the members of parliament. "I don't want to see the UMP turned into an applause machine. I don't want that. The party has to be free, free to say things, otherwise the President will be locked up and then it's over . . . I am not leading a political struggle. I am leading an ideological struggle. We have run a campaign on values. We are going to win by taking risks. I believe you take it all or take nothing. That strategy, is the only one that allows you to win. and I'm telling you that's the only one that allows you to be happy."

That afternoon, in Rouen, I tell him I was impressed by the way he handled the elected officials. He looks surprised. He doesn't feel entitled to praise for performances of this type. Still, it's often when, far away from microphones and cameras, he spreads, without thinking, the whole span of his freedom, that I admire him without qualification.

In Rouen. A good quarter of an hour (seems like three hours) on Joan of Arc. I mean to say on Joan. Joan only, Joan as France personified. The innocent, the martyr, the saint, the child of the people, calling out the name of Jesus among the flames, etc. Is there really any connection with the Nicolas Sarkozy that I know? . . . (Henri! Henri!! . . .)

Nathan:

"From time to time, in his speeches, he goes on a rampage with France. You see France arriving, like in history books in Africa. A huge woman, kind of flying, with a cape, and black people, arms outstretched, seeking happiness."

. . .

On TF1 and France 2, as hypothetical president, with a
new air of serene gravity (hint of sufferance).

". . .To see a parent suffering on what will soon be his
deathbed."

Piece of a phrase pronounced during the Arlette
Chabot show.

Clermont-Ferrand.

You know Yasmina Reza?

The furtively perplexed eyes of Valéry Giscard
d'Estaing, then: *Art*? I acquiesce.

Oh *Art,* it was superb! You've seen it, Nicolas, of
course?

Nicolas kindly praises me and adds, Right now she
is writing a portrait of me.

Ah! You're writing a . . .

A book, Mr. President, I say.

I see . . . a . . . a booklet?

Listening to him, after the meeting speaking in the
red-carpeted dressing room, with Valéry Giscard d'Estaing and other personalities, overhearing flattering
words, compliments, memories taken out of their
box, *the moralization of capitalism, you're the first one who*

spoke to me about it, people were telling me, what is that left-ist statement, and I would answer, From VGE's mouth to my ears, elbowing my way through people to recover a jacket, I suddenly think these are the last moments, in a week there will be no more buffet tables, chocolates, petitsfours, coffee machines that I don't know how to use, the dressing rooms more or less arranged, more or less cold, the screens badly tuned, the fake leather chairs, the makeup table, Marina's vanity case, the rolling wardrobe of suit and shirts, the photographs of the people standing next to the candidate one after the other, crazy with joy, the ties for the provinces, the tasseled shoes, the women with tassels, all those I embrace and who get me through the forbidden entrances, those who call out to me we are going and I have to hurry, in eight days all of that will no longer be.

He is speaking of a confidant. He says he is fragile. He says he is not solid. You can be solid and fragile. As a matter of fact, fragility is what makes solidity bearable.

I hear the last sentence as if he's addressing himself.

In Saint-Saulve, in the Vallouec factory producing nonwelded cast-iron tubes for the oil industry, I register the music of steel, the rumbling of deep voices, plaintive, of the blowers, the sounds of the bells, the high-pitched bangs, the containers, the blocks, the railings, yellow, blue, red, aged, blackened, the burning-hot catwalks along which we make our way, wearing white hard hats, and from which I would never have seen, had it not been for this book, the incandescent rods running on black rails, rolling on tilted metal plates, the fireworks, the canals of steaming water, all that magnificent metallurgy.

At Le Bourget. Near the gate, laughing, holding each other by the arm, Jean-Louis in a shirt, jacket on shoulder, Nicolas in a suit, under a resplendent sun, in front of the waiting cars, embracing, conspiring, whispering things into each other's ear, Nicolas shows him a text message, Borloo peeks, mouthing it in a very low voice, they crack up, tapping each other's cheek, they're thirteen years old, Pal, you're perfect for President, and I'll play the Queen of England!

In the dressing room at Bercy, standing next to Faudel, the singer, watching the screen, he names, staggering with joy, all the celebrities appearing. Alain

Prost!* . . . Henri! Henri Salvador!† Charlotte Rampling! And who's the little blonde? . . . Bigard!‡ . . . Look, look at the people outside! Christian and Jean Reno!§ Basile! Marina, can you do my makeup here? . . . (Pecking at some chocolates.) Look, they removed rows of seats at the back to let more people come in! . . . Oh, Mr. So-and-so! Oh, him! Oh, her! . . . Hello, Candeloro!** . . . André Glucksmann!! . . . And Farrugia!†† You see, we still have the left! Johnny arrives, he says, You stole my dressing room! He's teasing. He really is the boy who stole Johnny's dressing room, and can't get over it.

Twenty minutes later, made-up, coiffed, dressed like a legitimate person, wrapped in the essence of his function, and impatient to make it shine, he goes onstage.

. . .

* French race car driver.

† French singer, born in Cayenne, French Guiana.

‡ Jean-Marie Bigard, French comedian, actor, and director who actively supported Sarkozy.

§ French actor who works in both French and English and has appeared in many successful Hollywood productions.

** Philippe Candeloro, French figure skater who medaled at the 1994 and 1998 Winter Olympics.

†† Dominique Farrugia, French comedian of the left who is a member of Les Nuls.

Pierre Sarkozy enters the dressing room. He waits, at a distance, for his father to be freed up from a fan. As soon as he can, he approaches, presses his arm discreetly and, as he embraces him, in a low voice:

Bravo, Dad.

Among the people who are talking loud, among so much praise and demonstrative effusion, the tact and the loving modesty of his two older sons is gripping.

On the "Rebound" page of *Libération,* April 30, a column titled, "For Ségolène Royal, against Nicolas Sarkozy," and subtitled: "a call by intellectuals from the Left before the second round of the presidential election."

I forgo the weakness of the text, low-hanging fruit, to concentrate my interest on the signatures. A hundred names or so, mostly writers, directors, actors, moviemakers, musicians, or simply "artists." How uncanny for people whose eccentricity is the raison d'être, whose freedom and sometimes glory consist in having evaded reasonableness, to shoulder with such furious gravity the status of intellectual?

A picture. Seashore and pedal boats as backdrop. It could be called "work session with the new generation." An image of studious relaxation, in Corsica, for this last week of the campaign. Walking on the board-walk, on the pier in Cala-Rossa, Eric Besson asks me if it is the same in the Socialist Party, everyone sticking with the hero. I reply, of course (in fact, he stays so far from him that Nicolas will summon him). It is cold, it has been raining steadily. Rachida Dati, Valérie Pécresse,* Nathalie Kosciusko-Morizet,† Michèle Alliot-Marie, Brice Hortefeux, Claude Guéant, Xavier Bertrand, François Fillon, Eric Besson are present. If he is elected, they will be Ministers. They pretend to be at ease in their summer outfits. Pretend to contemplate the open sea in the secret of their soul. I am standing behind Élodie, who is taking the photo. I am wearing the charming flowered oilcloth raincoat that I had onstage for *In the Toboggan* . . . Xavier says, Yasmina without further ado fashioned herself a coat from a shower curtain!

A few words handpicked during the lunch:
MICHÈLE: (speaking of X.) He is self-involved. Maybe too much. It's not helping him.

---

* French politician, current Minister of Higher Education and Research, reportedly known as the Ségolène Royal of the right.

† French politician and member of the UMP, the Secretary of State in charge of ecology under Jean-Louis Borloo, the Minister of Ecology.

NICOLAS: Yes, but Michèle, in politics we're all self-
involved.

NICOLAS: You drive for miles and miles and in the
end you have a guy who says to you, And
what about the subsidies for ewes?

NICOLAS: If I win, I am going to outlaw the National
Front, the Lyon's Club, and the Rotary
Club.

NICOLAS: (repeating a sentence from his Bercy
speech) Between Jules Ferry and May '68,
they chose May '68 . . . Well, that verges on
dishonesty . . .

Y.: I'm glad to hear you say that . . .

NICOLAS: (laughing) Yeah. It's so dishonest, it's
terrifying, but then, the show must go on!

In the afternoon, in the sun, looking at the sea, open
shirt, neck chain, Joe Pesci dark glasses: "Listen to me,
Madame, you never managed a major crisis in your
entire career . . ." *Madame* is Xavier Bertrand, who is
super silly as Ségolène Royal, mute, acute, mocking:
"Mr. Sarkozy, for one, you're telling us thirty-five
hours is the full workweek, when, in fact, it is thirty-

eight . . ." Nicolas leans his head back against the tree trunk behind, asks what there is to drink, and argues with amicable precision. Eric Besson is a Madame Royal once removed, visibly torn and obstinate, receiving insulting text messages concerning his betrayal, because as this scene unfolds, an article in *Le Monde* discloses his presence in Corsica to prepare for the debate. Nicolas answers his opponents and adds, Nice weather, isn't it? It interests him and at the same time it bores him to death. He vacillates. He wavers between radically rejecting it and any possible benefit. I have often observed these pockets of inertia, land mines against any infiltration, against constraint. Fillon is attacking him about the education system's teaching hemorrhage. He immediately gets carried away. Bertrand goes further on the hospital issue. "Madame, Madame, please, explain to the French people how one can get better health care while spending less, please go ahead. We need money for hospitals, but where will that money come from? I'm talking about it, you're just not happy with what I'm saying. I'm creating resources for health care, you're not happy, you're never happy, stupid bitch! Tell me, where does your money come from? A dear old friend of mine, Madame, who has recently lost his hearing, his name is Jacques, we have to raise money for his hearing aid! . . ."

May 1.

Why the fuck are we going to some bleak operational center, to look at a radar? Did you guys check the weather forecast—is it rain or rain? Which retard came up with this idea? . . . I don't give a shit about Brions. It's going to be ten assholes and me, looking at a map! Half an hour to get to an operational center, and then another half an hour to go to the Alzheimer center! The crucial days of the campaign, in a room, looking at a map! . . .

A huge mural map of the Finistère. The words "helicopters," "British," "volunteer work," "Guernsey" buzz around his stiffened face. Beyond the windows, the sea of Iroise, the rain, the low sky. On a stony path, in the distance, among the rocks and the sparse grass, a little demonstration with eight people (circled by an equal number of gendarmes), is moving ahead, holding signs, Ségo—yes, Sarko—no.

In Bourg-Blanc, the reception at the Alzheimer treatment center.

On the wall in the hallway, some photographs of

the "outings": Visit to the Wrack Harvesters Museum in Plouguerneau, then snacks in Korejou Harbor. People, on a windy, sunny day, a little bent over, wearing checked pants, knit jackets with large buttons.

"We are now moving on to the garden, which is actually a therapeutic garden."

On a wooden bench sit five patients, four of them women.

NICOLAS: How long have you been here?

A WOMAN: On this bench?

NICOLAS: No, in the center!

Once Nicolas has passed by, they rise and take the graveled path, laughing. The man walks, doubled over.

The therapeutic garden is empty.

Élodie and I perch on the abandoned bench. We each hold a little bouquet of lilies of the valley from Frédéric Della Vale, bodyguard number one. We imagine we could be here one day. Facing this patch of soil where rhododendrons bloom. So depressing, says Élodie. A man passes by and informs us there are still a few rooms available. We have a laugh. It is my birthday. By the house entrance, there is a painted mural with a struggling workhorse and a dolmen, and a cross by the sea. Bright colors, circled by a black line. From inside comes the amplified voice of the one we're following. A man attempting to elevate himself in the world's eyes and whom the world might soon acclaim. What does he have to say to these people, sitting, frail, around a breakfast table, the last one they will see in their lifetime, in front of bowls, plates, bread, the realm of the ordinary that keeps shrinking. He doesn't say anything to them, he barely acknowledges them, he speaks to others, to those far away through the camera. The *maison basse* of Bourg-Blanc is a set, the patients are extras. In my notebook, this definition, without a source, of life as an exhausting struggle, in the end mortal, of life against itself. So depressing, repeats Élodie. I think of that scene, one of the most brilliant of all literature, Thomas Bernhard, the narrator, and Paul Wittgenstein, his friend, are sitting on a bench after meeting again between the Hermann Pavilion for the consumptives and the Ludwig Pavilion for the lunatics of the Steinhof, each of them in the uniform of his respective ward. *We were sitting on a bench, one of those, which still belonged to the lung ward. Grotesque! Grotesque! he said, upon which he started to cry without being able to stop.*

He says this, on the way back from Britanny, My past is a stranger to me. The only thing that interests me is this afternoon, tomorrow.

I ask him why not *right now*. I say, The present never interests you, you live in a perpetual becoming. He considers. He concurs. I say, You sacrifice instants that will never return, you are burning days unknown to yourself.

He says, Yes.

In his office on rue d'Enghien. Alone, facing Pierre Giacometti, head of Ipsos. Claude Guéant is here and silent.

Pierre Giacometti informs him about the last poll (53 percent of voter intentions) and talks about the balance of Bayrou voters having shifted in the right direction.

NICOLAS: So you're sure?

PIERRE: Yes.

NICOLAS: We can rack up a decent score?

PIERRE: That's what debates are for.

Silence.

NICOLAS: I'm really getting hammered.

PIERRE: That's a good thing.

Silence.

NICOLAS: I refuse to engage. People are losing their cool over this debate. It's absurd. They need to chill.

Silence.

PIERRE: The less you interrupt her, the better. I
think we want to go receptive, relaxed,
respectful on this.

Nicolas approves silently, reading what Pierre just
gave him. He is stretched out, jacket off, legs on the
coffee table, alongside three arrangements of lilies of
the valley.

Pierre Giacometti knows that he is speaking to a man
who doesn't like to be spoken at. He expresses profes-
sional opinions and limits himself to the essentials.

PIERRE: At the end of the day, you leave them with
the thought that you respect the left.

NICOLAS: Yes.

PIERRE: The French people think that she is out of
touch with reality. You are concrete. *Say to
us, spell out for us.* I recommend you use *us*.

NICOLAS: Okay. (Pause.) That's it.

PIERRE: Good.

Silence.

NICOLAS: Bayrou?

PIERRE: We can't rule out that he might speak on
Thursday or Friday.

NICOLAS: He's going to say that we're two boobs, I
don't care. I'm glad I said that thing about

the French Open, how you never see guy
number three in the finals. It was a heavy
serve, but it felt so good.

Long silence.

NICOLAS: Okay. I know what I have to do. I just have
to do it.

The next evening, head to head with Ségolène Royal,
he does just that.

On the way to Plateau des Glières, final campaign
appearance, I complain to Henri about the nostalgia
haloing the most recent speeches and the delirious ref-
erences to spirituality. He graciously receives this crit-
icism as a compliment.

I have felt close to monks . . . had they dared, the day
before, in Montpellier.

You've felt close to monks? I ask Nicolas.

Yes, very close to monks! . . .

And *this long mantle of cathedrals . . .* was it you or
Henri?

It was me. I added that.

I ask his sister, who's accompanying us, if he has
always been close to monks and cathedrals. She rolls
her eyes.

Women are so stiff, he says.

. . .

He thumbs through the papers scattered around; they are all predicting his victory. "I will have a palace in Paris, a castle in Rambouillet, and a fort in Brégançon. That's the way it will be."

Throwing away *Les Échos,* a headline to his advantage, after the debate with Royal: "I don't know why I read all this, why I'm reading all this shit!"

He has already won. A victory announced in the dismal dramaturgy of print, distilled by all the noise makers, a fate predicted, an obscure magic he tries to preserve.

Road, so beautiful, from the Plateau des Glières to the Petit Bornand. Craggy mountains against that soft white sky. Beech, ash, tender green, among the pine, hamlets of wood and stone, torrents, austerity of the coming spring.

Far away from it all.

In the village inn, back to back, seated at different tables, eating *fondue savoyarde,* they lean back onto each other:

HENRI: During the campaign, you've only gotten better.

NICOLAS: I hope you keep getting better, until you're
as good as me.

A crowd-pleaser, a shtick, which, in its acidic honesty (the insane shamelessness of the one, the lucid and cruel intentions of the other), pulls back the curtain to reveal the opposite of what was intended, scattering spores of half-hidden tomorrows.

"I don't like to depend and I don't like to be depended on."

Another time, he says to me, I understand the principle of being on tour and then going back to your life.

And countless other sentences picked randomly from the pages, about this inclination, this desire to emancipate oneself from others, to put oneself *out of reach*.

Sunday, May 6.

I say to his mother, Andrée, who is sitting in an armchair, in the office on the rue d'Enghien, with the rest of the family, brothers, sisters, children, guests on their best behavior, a few tolerated celebrities . . . I say to his mother, Your son was just elected President of the Republic, I have been watching you for five minutes, you're calm, quiet. Oh, you know, she says, nothing will move me nearly as much as the day he was elected in Neuilly, he was only twenty-seven years old.

I reread my notes of the day. The overcrowded room, the precedences—when Alain Juppé arrives, Nicolas calls upon—no kid gloves treatment—a few people to give up theirs chairs, the joyless announcement of the results. "Things are shaping up well, the French people trust us," the reading of the declaration in an even voice, the advice to the politicians, saying that victory binds us, saying that we are going to keep our word . . . "We now have the parliamentary elections. Beware of seeming arrogant or insufficient, the French people have an ingenious way of leaning to the center," the office transformed into a cocktail lounge, those invited to sneak in, those milling about outside the door, the mechanical embraces, the posed photographs, the countdown in chorus, the face appearing on-screen at 8:00 p.m., the bravos as if he had blown out his birthday candles, the calls from Chirac, from Omar Bongo ("A big hug for my Omar!"), from Ségolène Royal (eavesdropped on by me as a pathetic gossip, glued to the partition meant to provide for privacy), crossing Paris to go to Salle Gaveau,* the crazed motorcade, the police, the photographers, the TV cameras, the drunken procession of the cars that follow (I ride, surreally, in one), the dull, pensive, face, seen through a window, the dressing room at Gaveau, the embrace, a real one, with Frédéric Della Vale ("my friend, my brother"), of whom he once said, He never says a word, the private tears of sons Pierre and Jean, the social event at Fouquet's, the fury of cell phones, the coldness of the night at Place de la Concorde, the congratulations that I don't understand at all, the desolation of the noise, the desolation of the caravans, the cables crawling behind the stage, the barriers being moved, the waiting for the man who doesn't show up, lost somewhere in the excitement.

> *Captain, your eager cares were all deceits,*
> *(. . .)*
> *Time has the conquests, man has the defeats.*
> *The steel that was to wound you fell to rust;*
> *And you (as we shall be) are turned to dust.*
>
> —Jorge Luis Borges
>   "On the Effigy of a Captain in Cromwell's
>   Armies"

* Classical-music hall in the eighth arrondissement of Paris that features chamber music and private events.

. . .

An account by Samuel:

"I felt like a complete stranger in the jubilant crowd. I feel like a stranger in these crowds. I couldn't find a taxi, they were all full, I walked the quays and I realized how close rue de Solférino* was to Place de la Concorde. Only the Seine separated them. I came to the corner of rue de l'Université, at a café called Solférino. The café was closing. Some Ségolène supporters were coming out, completely destroyed, mute, dazed. I couldn't understand the euphoria, or the despair, I felt like an alien. There was a city truck, a street cleaner sweeping the sidewalk covered with refuse, papers, cartons, like a street market had ended. I went up boulevard Saint Germain, passing the Maison de l'Amérique Latine, there was another group, of more chic champagne socialists, like ghosts, chagrinned. Hungry, I reach the door of Brasserie Lipp, which is closing, the lights are on, the guy is counting the till, the waiters cleaning tables. Same at Deux-Magots.

At Place de la Concorde, I was onstage with him, in the back, in the background, just to see the crowd that, before, I had only heard. It was difficult to see people,

* Location of the Socialist Party's headquarters.

you could only make out the first ten meters that were lit. At this point, I became aware of, very humbly, mostly for the boss, the obligation. I understood the enormous burden. I didn't listen to the speech, I was already in the *after*. I thought, He reinvented politics with the right words, and now is the time for action. He is the only one who can do it. We have done the groundwork, but these are only preliminaries, now a whole new battle starts. My anxiety is based on that. Did I make a mistake with this man? Is he the one?

I was chosen for my competence and I chose him, when I saw he had the political courage to defend what was technically right. I really discovered politics, for the first time, in 1998. I was a gendarme and I met Paul Quilès,* who said something that shook me. "What is technically right may not be politically viable." When you are raised in a system where everything leads to the duty of self-sacrifice—I went to Saint Cyr rather than ÉNA,† to save my country—and a dry guy tells me abruptly that sacrifice is meaningless if not coupled with a political dimension, it's a culture shock. I understood that politics is both a constraint

---

* Senior member of the Socialist Party.

† The École Nationale d'Administration is the school where many of France's senior officials study.

and an opportunity. And that he had the courage to ensure that these dimensions coexist. What I understood from the boss was his sense of freedom."

Didn't he say, For a few days, I'll think, rest, retreat. I must prepare myself to occupy this place. I need calm and serenity to find the necessary distance. So close to the monks and the cathedrals, didn't he pride himself on some sudden transfiguration? Didn't he say, I'll find an abbey, or the solitude of some friendly house, to meditate on the magnitude of the task?

He will next be seen on a two-hundred-foot yacht, moored in front of Malta, devouring lobsters with his family.

In the Luxembourg garden, there are black people, white people, I say to myself, Oh, there are Jews too (I mistake a shiny jelled head for a yarmulke), and there is a half-caste, our President-elect, Nicolas Sarkozy. Too tanned for his first outing, a good three feet from Jacques Chirac, still holding high function, listening to a revolutionary song of 1794, "The Freedom of the Negroes," he contemplates, curiously frozen, the disconcerting interlacing that is the sculpture called *Oeuvre,* commemorating slavery and its abolition.

.   .   .

Under the noon sun, tracing the circle of those present, the Presidents shake hands. The elected President offers his hand to me, and I shake it. He is another person, and so am I.

Ivan quotes for me a confidante of Mitterrand: "To accede to the supreme office, one must desire it, love it, and finally will it." And he comments immediately, of course, only the *will* really matters. I am troubled by the truth of these words. Those of Mitterrand and those of Ivan. Keeping close to Nicolas during these months, I have seen only *will* at work. The desire for, the attraction to politics, principles so vital as to mobilize a whole being, no longer live in him. They were his matter in a period I never knew and which he never ceases to rue.

How weird to will *at any cost,* at the cost of the weightiest renouncements, something that no longer excites, that one no longer loves. Forsaken by forms most vital, the will remains. The will as residue. Still so powerful.

G. is playing. He takes a beating. He's hurt, but he's having fun too. I say to him, What do you want to do with your life now? He replies, That's the question. Because G. desires, loves, and might not be willing.

. . .

Thumbing through the notebooks—they're mumbling about old times—I stumble on this phrase: "We might end up winning after all." The last two words are circled.

After all, he is now President of the French Republic.

He called on his return from Malta.

I wanted to say hi, Yasmina. I wanted to say how happy having you along on this campaign has made me. I thank him and add, You remember our agreement? He says, yes. Remember that I will follow you around until the end of June? He says, Stay as long as you like.

Another life begins, Philippe Ridet writes in *Le Monde.* A life that goes on without Laurent, without Jean-Michel, without Frédéric. And without Élodie.

When the prince becomes king, José Frèches says to me, those who have seen the prince cry are sent to the salt mines. Since the dawn of times.

Have I seen the prince cry?

I see him again on May 16, his first day in the Élysée palace.

In the palace ballroom, under large chandeliers, confined behind a protective rope, guests are waiting. The Conseil d'État, the diplomatic corps, the Cour des Comptes, all sorts of brotherhoods, congregations, politicians packed in clusters, personal guests, family, acquaintances from the business world, cultural contacts, journalists coming out of the woodwork, all wait patiently. A man stands apart, not because of his geographic position, but his emaciated face, tragic, his abnormal stiffness in front of the microphone, his bitter and blanched solitude, the President of the Conseil Constitutionnel, in charge of the proclamation of the results of May 6, Jean-Louis Debré.* Look how overjoyed he is, Glucksmann says, he is contemplating a France he did not plan. Enter Cécilia in an ivory Prada, accompanied by Louis, her daughters, and the President's elder sons. After greeting a few guests effusively, she takes her place alongside the children, to the right of an empty stand. She is ravishing, the children are ravishing, glossy, enjoying being exhibited. He arrives. Stops behind the stand. The heroic Debré manages to produce out of a larynx paralyzed for the last hour: ". . . You are embodying France, you are the

---

* Also President of the Assembly, the most loyal of all Chirac loyalists; Debré never accepted Sarkozy as the new President.

symbol of the Republic, and you represent every French citizen . . ." A general presents him with the grand collar chain of the Ordre National and the Légion d'honneur. He seizes the massive case and inspects the links, looking a little bewildered. He marches toward his paper prompts, his first presidential address . . . *Necessity to respect the word given and the promises made . . . Necessity to restore the values of work, of effort, of merit, of respect* . . . Words from the campaign, which seem to me strangely calcified, *Morality . . . dignity . . . tolerance . . . justice . . . fraternity . . . love* . . . Words, likely to create a lyrical illusion in a process of movement and effort in themselves, feel frozen, emptied of their virtuous substance. (My friend Marc, who supported him publicly, will tell me the next day, Another two weeks of speeches on duty and respect, and I'll go over to the extreme left.) A calcification of the speech, which could, on this day, in the pomp of this place, in front of a pit that is already a court, correspond to a calcification of his being. Even though this perspective is, so to speak, an aberration. Still, it is another person that I see in profile interpreting his solemn mission; saying his rosary of demands he fancies he is a depositary, another person, supported by a united family, twinkling, shining, shaking hands above the rope with people, smiling, bowing, thanking for everything, for nothing, because he doesn't owe anything to anyone and he knows it, another person, now racing toward his first day as leader of the nation, exercising, with favorites new and newly appointed, a modern king in an old castle, and the dry thought occurs that this is the last circumstance in which I will see him in his pomp, at close range, for real, as children say. A contact brutally severed. *Stay as long as you like.* Actually, no.

The restaurant Farnesina, at 2 p.m., I watch the President of the Republic, on a friend's cell phone, go down the Champs-Élysées in his convertible car. On his feet, hand raised, police escorted, he is so small in Jean-Pierre's hand, and I must place the phone against my ear to hear the cheers.

I am calling you, Yasmina, to tell you that you are a member of the delegation going tomorrow to the Airbus site at Méaulte. I decline. I explain once again to the chief of staff, what I have said the day before to Claude, now secretary general of the Élysée, that I will no longer accompany Nicolas Sarkozy.

During the news, I see footage of the appearance. The first one in French territory. I see the President and his

Minister of Finance, Jean-Louis Borloo, moving at top speed along the cockpits, stopping like in the past to watch something being adjusted, waving like in the past at employees in another huge, clean hangar. I see him like in the past at the roundtable with the unions, in front of the A310 model, moody, agitated, I notice tics I know, I think the day must be long, tiresome, I see him from my home, and I listen, in this montage of image and sound, to the intonations, like in the past, to a recorded broadcast like everyone else.

That evening, the new chief of staff calls to tell me that the President wants to see me.

What do you think? A little dull, huh?

We are alone in his office. The office of the President of the French Republic, at the Élysée. A year almost to the day after our first meeting at the Ministry of the Interior. Across the street (as he enjoyed putting it).

I got rid of a lot of stuff Chirac left. There was a big horn of a . . . (he gestures).

Of a rhinoceros?

No . . . You know the guys in the water, who have a horn . . . You see? . . . (I don't see and he can't find the word) . . . Do you want a coffee, an orange juice?

He is seated on a gilded banquette and I on a gilded

armchair. Between us, a narrow coffee table, Chinese.
Everything is gilded, gilded curtains, gilded moldings,
gilded tapestries.

I say: "Are you content?"

"This is the word you chose?"

"I am not going to say happy."

"I am serene."

"Serene is good."

"Yes. Deep inside, I'm content, but there is no joy."

He has stretched his legs out. I'm not sure that this
banquette is suited for him. In the room, three bou-
quets of peonies, white and pink.

I keep silent. I could say, Why did you want to see
me, but I don't say it. He could say, Why do you want
to stop, but he doesn't say it. What for? We know
the answers and any kind of explanation would be
demeaning.

We speak therefore of . . . politics. The new government. Mr. So-and-so. Mrs. So-and-so. Suddenly, he
gets up, grabs a little piece of modern furniture, half
stool, half bedside table, which is near a window, and
without any apparent reason goes to align it against
the opposite wall. Then he comes back and sits. I say,
That's crazy what you just did. He says, You think so?

He smiles to me silently like in the past when there
was nothing hurrying, in dressing rooms, in planes,

waiting. In intermediary places where immobility doesn't equal death, on the contrary, just a place where you catch your breath. He used to come, he would say to me, to this office as an impetuous visitor. He wasn't the one who stayed, looking through the windows, on the deserted lawn, and, to the back, at the interminable jet of water.

G. lists for me the names of the cities where he goes. They are not names of cities, but names of days, of dates, mooring posts in an endless circle that men invent for themselves in order to flee from the idleness of what would be otherwise pedestrian; elections, committees, congresses, universities, where one has to swell the ranks of the busybodies, to persist in the glaring light that bestows a future, because there is no other life.

Seated, at the end of a banquette with the large backdrop of the wallpaper, and had the picture been in black and white, the one who, from now on, inhabits these premises, would make me think of a composition of Diane Arbus, victorious boy, frozen, alone, under a sky of garlands. Shoulders slightly drooping under the well-cut white shirt, abandoned in a tranquil stupor, extending no effort to attract. Thumbed through *Revelations* again, the extraordinary album of Arbus. Assortment of solitudes, compilations of fragile lives on flower-print sofas, on park benches, on the edge of empty beds, bogged-down bodies, waiting for nothing, in spite of the paraphernalia of finery and getup, infernal hairdos, and that is exactly, I say to myself, what the men I speak of are fleeing, the place where there is nothing to wait for, the old days in tatters, the monotonous train of no conclusion, the existence extinguishing unseen.

Words of Didier: "Women are happy when they wriggle. Us, what do we have, we have the remote control. We don't have eyeliner, the bag, all those things that add color, it's a hell of a job being a woman. We don't have that, we are more prone to battling boredom, pressed by time, speeding along, pedal to the metal."

The President leaves. (I stay on the same floor because I want to see Henri, who occupies the office next door.) He exits, putting on his jacket. He is rushing. He is bolting. I see him walking, his back, turning for a last wave, checking his pockets, the cell phone, disappearing through the door frame with a light limp. Quickening the pace, I say to myself, as soon as the jacket is grabbed off the back of the gilded armchair, to escape God knows where, slipping the arm in the sleeve, his wriggling to do so a testimonial to life. He has to leave, to go out, to foil (to spoil) the encircling of walls, their silent maneuvers.

Before he disappeared, I had said, I wanted to ask you something. Yes? I would like you to grant me what you never have. What? A real conversation.

Saturday, June 2.

Come, come, Yasmina!

I follow him in his office. He closes the window.

I didn't notice that you had a balcony.

Me, neither.

I am sitting, in the same place. And he on his banquette:

"I cannot tell you that I am unhappy . . . Here it is, I finally got rid of that burden . . ."

He is in jeans. While speaking, he is cleaning his watch with a white handkerchief.

"To win is to seduce," he says. "My job is to decide. I was much more worried about my capacity to seduce."

He has tamed the banquette, I say to myself, he is satisfied with its conventionality and lack of comfort.

.   .   .

In the silent salon, the notebook wisely posed on my lap, no possible mishap, every word uttered atrophies.

Sitting, seeing each other in the silent salon, confined to the reasonable, when movement was what prompted the writing.

No grace period, he says (I believe him) while the papers only speak of it. I look at him, face leaning over the Rolex bracelet, taking pains over his task, taking pains over the choice of authentic words, as requested by me. An application to being, a seriousness, that I knew him to have through all these months, where, in spite of the showiness, the convivial manner, or the laughing enthusiasm, there was not a trace of frivolity, that expansion of joy essential to grace.

One year since the day I thanked him for receiving me, expecting a refusal, expecting at best an I'm going to think about it, and certainly not that immediate Yes. In my first notes of the first notebook, I read the prophetic enumerations, Agen, June 22, 2006—make-up—cell phone—security—speed—no dead time—not a second in place, except for photos—childish demeanor—chocolate—candied fruit squares—pecking—pecking—laughing—*I want to live,* he says in the ultimate office, during this "real conversation," I ask, what does that mean? On a double page of the *Paris Match* of the week after his election, there is a photograph of him, in black and white, on a bicycle in Vesoul, dating back to November 2001. In cyclist shorts, hunched in a puffed Windbreaker, he is riding, head turned toward the lens. He is smiling, a graceless yet strikingly happy smile (like the one of children whose form is not yet polished for seduction), he is pedaling, he is rolling, he doesn't want to know anything else. I cannot extract anything from this real conversation, I mean nothing for the writing. The Saturday jean, the curve of the body on the banquette, the cleaning of the watch, the details dimly lit of the man fascinate more than words.

They say Ulysses, wearied of wonders,
wept with love on seeing Ithaca,
humble and green. Art is that Ithaca,
a green eternity, not wonders.

—Jorge Luis Borges
  "The Art of Poetry"

One day, on the road, headed for Marseille, Patrick Devedjian told me: "Power is like the horizon, the closer it gets, the farther away you are. But you have to see the landscape behind the mountain. Maybe it is Ulysses' voyage. Gone like him in search of his origins. The presidential election, it's Ulysses' voyage."

I had noted those seductive surmises.

Origins? What native country wouldn't be the one of oblivion and indifference? Neither the places nor the days lingered. Stranger to my past, he had said. Born on a soil that means nothing and is nowhere, and no Ithaca to return to. No green, no plain, no green eternity. I understand, though, the nostalgia one could feel. *To see, if only, the smoke rising from his land . . . so true it is that nothing is sweeter than native country and kin.* A nostalgia without recourse. Behind the mountain, the memory of a time of wonders, the fleeting trace of a sparkle, but no smoke, no green meadow, and it isn't sure there's anything at all.

Acknowledgments

My great thanks to Nicolas Sarkozy for the freedom he granted me.

To Cécilia Sarkozy, who approved this project.

My most particular thanks to Laurent Solly.

And Élodie Grégoire.

Also Jean-Michel Goudard, Samuel Fringant, Franck Louvrier, Pierre Charon.

My thanks to David Martinon, Michel Besnard and his team.

And to Hugues Moutouh.

To all those I have no space to mention, who took care of me during all these months, in Paris or on all the many campaign trips.

To all the unlucky people who had to find my lost cell phone, my glasses, my makeup bag, and so on . . .

To all the photographers and journalists who were following Nicolas Sarkozy during the campaign and respected my requests for privacy.

Pierre Guglielmina and I wish to thank Ilsa Carter for her wit and her inspired suggestions.

And last of all, last but not least, I would like to thank my friend Nicole Garcia for all the conversations that kept me going.

A NOTE ON THE TYPE

This book was set in a version of the well-known Monotype
face Bembo. This letter was cut for the celebrated Venetian
printer Aldus Manutius by Francesco Griffo, and first used in
Pietro Cardinal Bembo's *De Aetna* of 1495.

The companion italic is an adaptation of the chancery
script type designed by the calligrapher and printer Lodovico
degli Arrighi.

Composed by Creative Graphics, Inc.,
Allentown, Pennsylvania

Printed and bound by R. R. Donnelley & Sons,
Harrisonburg, Virginia